PUZZLES OF FAITH AND PATTERNS OF DOUBT

Short Stories and Poems

PUZZLES OF FAITH AND PATTERNS OF DOUBT
Short Stories and Poems

Edited By

GREGORY F. TAGUE

Bibliotekos
E♦B

New York

Bibliotekos
Finding the Uncommon Reader

Fredericka A. Jacks, Publisher

**Cover Photography (Carmelite Monastery, Dublin):
Mary Kenefick Keating**

Editorial Interns:
Evan Czmola, Tyler Perkins, and Kimberly Resnick

Printed & Bound in the United States

Set in Garamond

ISBN: 978-0-9824819-6-7

**Bibliotekos
E♦B
New York**

Anyone with any idea of what it means to live on spirit knows also what the hunger of doubt means, and that the doubter hungers just as much for the daily bread of life as for the sustenance of spirit.

- Søren Kierkegaard

CONTENTS

Preface,
Gregory F. Tague & Fredericka A. Jacks   ix

Foreword,
Rev. David Rommereim   xi

Larry Lefkowitz,
The Shoemaker   1

Patty Somlo,
Since Leticia Williams Saw Jesus   7

Arthur Powers,
Padre Raimundo's Army   15

Frank Russo,
In the Museum of Creation; Nativity of Christ Cathedral,
Riga; Blind Faith; Good Friday, Lake Victoria;
The Caves of Atapuerca   23

Rivka Keren,
Zipora   31

Michele Merens,
Hilde's Son, the Rabbi   37

Julie J. Nichols,
One Traveler   49

Atar Hadari,
The Empty Synagogue; Aroma; Honey; Mr. Taylor;
Prayers; High Windows; Healers; Silence   61

Gary Guinn,
The Scar   71

W.C. Bamberger,
In the Details   83

Andrea Vojtko,
Searching for Life on Mars   101

Bill Scalia,
Dawn, Day 1; When God Called Adam from the Dirt;
The Mass of Pallas Athena; Intercession (The Authenticity
Dream); The Revival; Vastation; The End of Time   111

Edie Cottrell,
Pumpkin Patch   119

Joey Dean Hale,
Access Closed   129

Roberta Allen,
Odd   137

Biographical Notes &
Publication Acknowledgments   143

About Bibliotekos   147

PREFACE

Gregory F. Tague & Fredericka A. Jacks

This collection begins and ends in the desert, and such a symbolic setting is appropriate, for the prophet Isaiah tells us that a voice cries out from the desert. Whose voice? We think of John the Baptist preaching in the desert and Jesus in the wilderness resisting the devil's temptations. Other religious and spiritual leaders have associations with the desert (Mohammed) or have led people literally or figuratively out of the desert (Moses, Buddha).

In part, the voice in the desert is our own. What do we say, and who will hear us? The book opens and closes with first-person narratives, characters searching for answers, and this too is appropriate: in the spiritual realm, we sometimes feel the only voice in the desert is ours, and hence the questions of what to believe and whom to believe in.

The working title for this anthology had been Faith and Doubt. But the more we considered the spiritual journey we realized that there is an incessant pattern of doubt always nagging, tearing at one; yet, faith is strong enough to be seen, to be felt, to be heard. But this faith is like an incomplete puzzle – there is always one piece missing.

Much of the work in this volume is not religious – the doubts that strain one's faith are questions of character, difficulties in personal relationships, or problems in the family. The puzzle of faith is not really about God, it's about the human predicament: our sins, our mistakes, our failures (and at times our glories) with ourselves and others.

FOREWORD

Rev. David Rommereim

Though I walk through the Valley of Shadow is a sliver of Biblical poetry that engages many in the Judeo Christian movement. It touches the heartstring of deep memory when we wander off into the puzzle of faith and enter the wild nature of doubt. Even with the persistent menace of a benign atheism that captivates our anxious culture, the self and other grasp hands. They hold one another and stumble together over the presentiment of certainty and its nemesis ambivalence. Each yearns for a difference beyond what is polarized as the real and the mysterious. Each of us meanders toward a home that seeks to share the awe and its incense of an abiding confidence.

The poetry and stories in this wonderful volume shaped by Gregory Tague and Fredericka Jacks remind me that it was when I said "I believe" that I entered that thin space between certainty and ambiguity. When I read the stories aloud, I began to see my faith staring at me like a mirror, with all the wrinkles and crusty wear that my life has offered.

This collection animates my little fingers touching the threadbare material of faith and doubt. These poems and stories remind me of the courage it takes to open my eyes to the things that give life and allow me to notice what is right before my face. This observation, I believe, gives us ability to withstand the awesome experience of mystery and its kindred spirit we have named faith.

Faith grips the thread that separates the two forces of the soul. One hand embraces the plot passed to us from the ancestry of faith, generations we have only met in the common experience of communal living. Another hand grips the delicate thread that offers the audacity to move forward in the journey even when our community struggles with the continuity of values and meaning.

In this volume, you will notice those who have risked observing their living with the delicate venture into what is other. You will wander in the wilderness of the pain caused by misinformed choices. You will see those who turn hallucination into healing. You will enjoy the turning of death from empty religion into the raw gift of grief. You will pay attention to the packages offered in the stories that announce the timely gift of reconciliation and forgiveness; hope from the places of deep pain re-imagined and healed through the telling. Each describes what is beyond the ordinary, as well as what is deeper in the vicissitudes of a faith moving well beyond religion and into the heart songs which religion hopes to honor, but has become limited by its penchant to be above doubt and beyond mystery.

These stories and poems are individuals who will surprise you with the divine mystery and the drama of moral courage sometimes thwarted, sometimes embellished, always noticed when one stops to read and watch.

The Shoemaker

Larry Lefkowitz

It was soon known in the neighborhood that the shoemaker left his wife and children. Rumors abounded as to why and where he went. Varied and imaginative they were – even that he went to look for the hidden place of the Ark of the Covenant. All of the rumors placed him in the desert because the reported sightings of him had him heading south. But as to exactly where in the desert, no one agreed. Some placed him in the caves near Qumran – perhaps because his wife said that shortly before he disappeared, she heard him murmur over and over: "The wars of the children of light against the children of darkness." Others placed him in the cliffs above Ein Gedi.

His wife, who was known to refer to him even before he abandoned her, as "the eccentric" or "the crazy one," depending upon her charity, after a year met a man, moved in with him and, after another year without a sign of her husband's returning, married him.

Three years later the shoemaker returned, seemingly uncaring whether his wife had remarried, and ignored his children whom his wife had raised to avoid him. Any questions as to his whereabouts during the previous three years he dismissed angrily; in any event because of his quick-to-anger temperament, few dared ask him where he had been, or what he did there. Even the most persistent of neighborhood busybodies knew to hold their peace in the presence of the shoemaker. The saying, "If you don't want to be the sole of a shoe, don't antagonize the shoemaker," was common neighborhood coinage. Nobody called him by name; he was always "the shoemaker," as if to use his name was too personal, evincing a familiarity that could be dangerous. There was something about him of a prophet of wrath – except that he didn't prophesize. Or if he did, we failed to grasp his prophecy.

Upon his return, the shoemaker shooed the cats out of their quarters and reopened his cobbler shop which had remained closed during his absence. No longer with access to his former living quarters (which his wife had sold when she moved in with her new husband), he slept on a mat on a narrow raised platform which he built above his work bench inside the shop, dubbed by the neighborhood wags as his "Procrustean bed." The shoemaker didn't have many customers, either because of his strangeness or because of his temperament or because he was far from being a master of his craft, and the customers that did frequent his shop did so because it was located close to where they lived. Most of all, his prices were low.

From time to time, I gave him some business because I was curious about him and because I was drawn to the odor of leather and glue that filled the shop. He didn't mind if I lingered there without saying much. He usually had some tacks in his mouth, more, I suspected, as a defense against having to speak than as a work convenience. I didn't pester him with questions, adopting the strategy of silence, or indifference, which didn't help me much, though he tolerated, and eventually seemed even to enjoy, my presence. Maybe he just got used to me – like an old shoe.

One day, as he was working on the sole of my shoe, he uttered, more to himself than to me, "And ye shall tread down the wicked, for they shall be ashes under the soles of your feet," his hammering punctuating his avowal. And then he stopped, dropped his hammer on his workbench, spit out the tacks (an act which surprised and startled me), and began mumbling something about the rabbi from – he couldn't pronounce the name very well – one of those towns in Eastern Europe. An uncommon rambling on the shoemaker's part about a rabbi who one day astounded his disciples by entering his room and refusing to leave it for the rest of his life, dependent upon them to bring him food. Here the shoemaker paused as if wrestling with some thought and then, holding my glance in his, added something about how the presence of evil in the world might possibly have been too much for the rabbi's sanity to bear. "Trapped in a fortress of evil without anyone to ransom him."

I nodded and said nothing. What could I say?

Some days afterward, the shoemaker was gone again. A second time. The desert again? No one knew. Speculation nourished the neighborhood gossip in the following days. Someone said that before he left, he murmured over and over, "Dispersed to the place of the wicked to their subduing by fire." Toward the end of the same week, I heard a knock on my door. I opened it. A youth stood there, a pair of shoes in his hands. "From the shoemaker," he said. "I didn't leave him any shoes to be repaired," I told him. "He said they were a gift," the youth persisted. I glanced at the size written faintly inside the left shoe – it was my size. Although they had been polished to a bright sheen, the shoes were not new, and I surmised that somebody had left them to be repaired and failed to come back for them. But why look a pair of gift shoes in the mouth? They were expensive shoes. The shoemaker's from better days? Maybe his wedding shoes? I thanked the lad, and gave him some change. As he was about to leave, I grabbed his arm. "Tell me, do you know where the shoemaker went? His shop is closed." The boy shrugged, already thinking perhaps of what candy bars to buy with the coins I had given him.

I didn't get around to putting on the shoes for a couple of weeks, until my usual pair sprung a hole in the sole of one. As I put on the right shoe, I spied something inside. It was a folded piece of paper, which had been inserted in the toe portion of the shoe. I opened it. On it was written a single word: "Azaz." I repeated the word over and over, trying to fathom what it meant, this shoemaker's code delivered in a shoemaker's fashion. Finally, it rang a bell. Something about a scapegoat.

The "Azaz" wouldn't let go of me. It was as if the shoemaker was pushing me, to use the clue he had vouchsafed me, to solve the mystery of his disappearance. I began to delve into the subject.

I had been right about the scapegoat connection. The scapegoat was a goat that carried the sins of the people placed on it, designated "for Azazel," which was driven into the desert to perish as part of the ceremonies of the Day of Atonement. The rabbis of the time interpreted "Azazel" as "Azaz," which meant "rugged" and "el," which meant "strong." They considered that "Azaz" referred to the rugged mountain cliff from which the scapegoat was cast down. Others said it referred to the goat-like spirit haunting the desert to which the Israelites were accustomed to offering sacrifices. The shoemaker had a wispy, goat-like beard. Surely coincidence, but I found it disturbing nonetheless.

I never saw the shoemaker again. Nor did anyone else. Perhaps his one word message meant that he hadn't yet given up the search for the key to the presence of evil and his beholding with his own eyes "the recompense of the wicked." I was not a type to go on quests, even though the nature of evil often confounded me. Although it is forbidden to feel envy toward a poor, lost shoemaker, I felt envy: I had to live with the vexatious question of evil; the shoemaker had gone to try to decipher it and strive with it.

~

When I wake up at night and cannot sleep, the bad thoughts come. And so I, too, ponder the nature of evil in the world. Maybe for the shoemaker the days and the nights had become one.

Rashi said: "Satan prosecutes in the hour of danger" – that is, at such a time of danger he doesn't differentiate between the just and the wicked. Perhaps the shoemaker realized that the evil in himself or his attempt to uproot it impelled him to

4

be alone in the desert. To be "subdued by fire." The Ramban said that just as the fire intended to destroy, the thorns get out of control and destroy the crops, the evil inside of us must be restrained.

The shoemaker was not a person of restraint.

~

For days the shoemaker and his quest weighed heavily upon me. It did not lift until shortly before the Day of Atonement when I chanced (if chance it was) upon the story of how one day Rabbi Levi Yitzhak was asked by a poor shoemaker if he had something that needed fixing. The rabbi chastised himself, "You see, even he can see that I need to fix myself."

Which may explain why I continue to bring my shoes for repair to shoemaker shops outside of my neighborhood when it would be easier to buy a new pair of shoes.

Faith is to believe what we do not see; and the reward of this faith is to see what we believe.

St. Augustine

Since Leticia Williams Saw Jesus

Patty Somlo

Leticia Williams shook hands with Jesus on her very last day of rehab. The handshake occurred an hour before group and moments after she'd finished combing her hair. She had taken an extra minute to admire her reflection in the mirror, pleased at how her cheeks had filled out and her eyes had cleared. About to turn around and take a last look to make sure she'd packed up all her things, Leticia Williams saw Jesus, standing behind her reflection in the far right-hand corner of the mirror.

The breath left her, almost as if she'd been punched in the stomach. At first, she feared those crazy dammed hallucinations she'd had back in detox were coming back. The only thing to do, Leticia knew, was to turn around.

Her back to the mirror, Leticia saw the wavy brown hair and the off-white robe she'd just seen reflected.

"You real, ain't ya?" Leticia asked.

The man who looked exactly like Jesus silently reached out his right hand.

"You Jesus," Leticia said.

Leticia exhaled the words, her heart having started rattling in her chest and her throat gone dry.

He smiled and nodded, his clean brown hair reflecting the light. Leticia could only stare.

"Oh," Leticia said. "You waitin' on me, ain't ya?"

Leticia stepped toward the man, her legs suddenly shaking. She reached her trembling hand out, sure that when she tried to touch Jesus' hand, he would exist only in her mind. She aimed her right arm parallel to the floor. Then she curled her fingers. The warmth of Jesus' flesh was all the proof she needed.

"You real," she said.

Breath rushed from her mouth. Words were nearly lost.

A smile edged out from the corners of Jesus' lips as he shook Leticia's hand. Leticia let him lift and lower her hand.

The next moment, Jesus was gone. Leticia pulled her hand back and studied it. She wondered what in heaven's name she ought to do now. Still staring at her hand, she silently asked herself what a woman was supposed to do after she had shaken Jesus' hand.

At first, Leticia was hesitant to tell a single soul, knowing how easy it could be to confuse a vision with one of those dammed crazy hallucinations. But after graduation, in the cafeteria, its walls hung with red and blue crepe paper, and colored balloons strung down from the ceiling, and everyone standing around in their best dresses and a couple of guys in suits, with little kids running around screaming, Leticia thought about the moment she'd shared with Jesus and smiled.

"What you glowin' for, Leticia Williams?"

Diane Larson was standing a little too close for Leticia's comfort. Leticia took a couple of steps back, as she gave Diane the once-over. Diane was wearing a white clingy dress Leticia figured the girl had worn when she was out hustling on the street. There was too much skin exposed at the top and bottom of the dress to be decent.

"I'm just happy," Leticia said and took a sip of fruit punch, thinking for the umpteenth time since getting up out of bed that she hadn't had a drink in seven months.

"Kinda strange to be happy and not be usin', huh?" Diane asked.

Leticia considered the question. She gave Diane the once-over another time. It bothered her that Diane, a white woman, talked like she was black. Diane had long red hair Leticia could tell she dyed at home and nice blue eyes. The skin around her mouth was starting to pucker and get lines.

"They's other stuff to be glad about," Leticia said.

"Yeah. Like movin' to our own apartments."

Without planning to, Leticia let out what had happened, when she was in her room finishing getting dressed.

"I had a visitor today," Leticia said.

Word spread that Leticia Williams had shaken hands with Jesus. It drifted around amongst the folks who'd made it all the way through the program. Then it seeped into stories shared by men and women still struggling to control the demons of drugs and drink. People standing outside the clinic smoking – before and after group – and the ones on Methadone who'd come for their daily dosing shared the news.

Marleena Wright was the first to ask Leticia for a meeting. She'd relapsed over the weekend and her counselor threatened that one more time and Marleena would lose her apartment.

"I was wondering," Marleena said to Leticia, as they streamed out of the large, brightly-lit office filled with old sagging couches and a couple of fat chairs, where their group met. Marleena caught a piece of the red satin blouse in her fingers Leticia had snagged on sale the week before at Ross, which made Leticia mad.

"What was you wonderin'?" Leticia asked, as soon as they got outside and moved away from the group congregating in front of the clinic.

Marleena's shoulder-length hair had been bleached so many times it looked like the woman had left it outside on a sizzling afternoon in July. The roots were growing back, black and hard. Leticia was tempted to ask Marleena if she had any idea what she looked like.

Before she did, Marleena pulled a cigarette out of her bag, pressed her lips around the filter, and lit the end with a green plastic lighter.

"I ain't got all day, Marleena. You wanna tell me what you was wonderin'."

Leticia had her hands on her hips and the red satin of her blouse winked in the sunlight. Her hair was straightened and neatly combed. She had large, dark brown eyes, cocoa-colored skin, and a long thin face. The high cheekbones drew attention to her eyes.

"I was wonderin' if maybe I could come talk to you. Sometime soon. Everybody's been saying that since you saw Jesus, you have some special healing powers. If I slide back one more time, that might be it for me."

~

Leticia wasn't sure how a woman might go about becoming a healer. But she'd been in and out of rehab so many times, talking to this and that counselor, it was easy to move over to the helping side. Minutes before Marleena arrived, Leticia lit seven candles and set them on the coffee table and the little T.V. trays she used as side tables in the one-room apartment. She turned on one lamp next to the bed.

"Oooh," was all Marleena said when she stepped inside.

Leticia gave Marleena a cup of jasmine tea after she told her to sit down in one of the two metal chairs at the little table where Leticia ate.

"So," Leticia said, when she sat down at the table across from Marleena. "What d'ya want to know?"

Marleena picked at the chipped dark purple polish on her index fingernail. Leticia could see that Marleena was shaking some, the way people did in group when they were still using. Marleena raised her head from studying her fingers and Leticia could see that the woman looked about to bawl.

"I . . . I, well, I just thought. I mean, I wondered. I mean, if you saw Jesus, well, then maybe you could teach me how."

The minute Marleena finished talking, she went back to messing with her fingernails.

Leticia wasn't sure how to respond. She didn't have a clue why Jesus had unexpectedly decided to show up in her life. And it wasn't like she had any kind of special connection, like she could just call Jesus up on the phone and say, "Hey, look Jesus. I got this friend Marleena, and she be needin' you right now."

Leticia could see that Marleena needed help to keep from sliding back into a life of using and hustling, a world she'd get lost in, until most of her teeth were gone and her cheeks had sunk in, and she'd ended up in jail, with half her mind gone. Leticia took in a deep breath and closed her eyes.

"Let us pray on it a minute," she said.

Leticia stretched both arms out on the table. Marleena stopped fussing with her nails and clasped each of Leticia's hands. Their hands, dark and light with the fingers entwined, made a nice pattern on the scratched fake-wood table.

Not surprisingly, Leticia wasn't sure what to be praying for. She was distracted by the shaking coming from Marleena's fingers.

But then a picture came into Leticia's mind of Marleena standing on the sidewalk next to the liquor store. Leticia remembered that she'd seen Marleena there when she was still drinking, in those big high sandals that looked like blocks under her feet and that bleached hair looking like the wind had just messed with it. In her mind, Leticia could see the sadness on Marleena's face, even though those red-painted lips of hers were smiling.

That's when Leticia asked Jesus if he might possibly come back. She explained to him in her mind that she wasn't asking for herself.

"You see, Jesus," Leticia silently pleaded. She didn't want Marleena to know that she couldn't just bring Jesus into the room whenever she wanted. "This girl, Marleena, she needs you, Jesus. If you show up, that might be all it takes."

A moment later, Leticia was startled from her thoughts.

"Oh, my," Marleena said.

"What is it?" Leticia asked.

"It's him," Marleena said. Her wide-open eyes were looking someplace behind Leticia's head. Her hands loosened from Leticia's grip.

"What d'ya see?" Leticia asked.

Marleena started to cry. She wiped the back of her knuckle

underneath her right and then her left eye.

"D'ya see somethin'?"

"Yes," Marleena said, running a finger under her nose that had started to drip. Leticia could see that the woman's fingers were shaking.

"Jesus," Marleena said, the name whispered, so that Leticia had to lean in close, to be sure that's what Marleena was saying. "Jesus. He's right there."

Leticia wondered if she ought to turn around and make sure Jesus was standing there. She started to swivel at the waist, her hands balanced on the table. But then she changed her mind.

"You might ask him to help you," Leticia whispered back. "Ask him to help you stay straight."

~

One by one, women from the program and then a handful of men came to see Leticia. On each visit, Leticia lit seven candles and turned off all the lights, except the one small lamp next to the bed. And every one of the people who came to Leticia seeking help had a moment, after holding Leticia's hands while she prayed, when Jesus appeared.

Leticia continued to keep her back to Jesus. She thought about it, sometimes when she was alone, blowing out the candles, the apartment dark and smoky. What if she turned around one evening and Jesus was gone?

Since the morning she had shaken his hand, Leticia hadn't had a glimpse of Jesus. But she'd also been blessed. Not a single one of those crazy hallucinations had occurred.

Of course, the clean and sober life was not always easy. Every time Leticia made a mistake in school – leaving the straightening solution on too long so the hair got brittle, or the razor going too close to the skin and causing the client to bleed – she had to clamp her jaw tight and grind her teeth to keep from screaming. There'd been incidents too, when Leticia had thrown the scissors and comb on the floor and stomped away and William, her teacher, needed to sit with her while she had a minor breakdown.

~

Jesus was nowhere to be found the night Leticia Williams relapsed. It was a man – a pure flesh and blood man – who was the cause. His name was Rodney and he had skin the color of hot fudge on a sundae before it mixes with the vanilla ice cream. He called Leticia, "Baby, baby," when they made love, and told her she had the most *be-u-tiful* eyes.

And then Leticia saw Rodney with his lips on Diane Larson's neck and his hands running all over her body. Leticia marched over to him on the sidewalk outside the clinic, as he ground Diane's ass into his groin and then started to sway, like they were dancing.

"What you doin' with that whore?" Leticia screamed at Rodney, standing practically on top of him.

Rodney looked up, still hanging onto Diane Larson.

"Ain't no business of yours," Rodney said.

"It sure is my business," Leticia said and grabbed Rodney by the arm.

"Get your hands offa me."

Rodney shoved Leticia back.

"Get away from me, bitch."

Jesus did not accompany Leticia when she sprinted straight over from the clinic to the liquor store. He did not sit with her as she gulped herself into a stupor. And the next morning, when she slept in, missing class at the beauty school, Jesus didn't bother to try and wake her.

In fact, that entire week, when Leticia barely ate and guzzled one bottle of thick, sweet red wine after another, Jesus didn't stop by. Leticia ignored the phone when it rang, so she couldn't be certain that Jesus hadn't called.

It was Marleena who got the landlord to open the apartment door. And it was Marleena who helped Leticia into the tub and washed her hair and face, her legs and arms, and helped her into some clean clothes. Marleena fed Leticia spoonfuls of chicken noodle soup and went with her the next morning to group. Marleena even stayed over a couple of nights, curled up on the couch, to make sure Leticia didn't go out and buy more wine.

One warm July evening, several weeks later, Marleena lit seven candles and turned off the lights. She stretched her arms across the fake-wood table in Leticia's apartment and waited for Leticia to grab her hands. Then she closed her eyes and prayed for Jesus to come to Leticia's aide.

Leticia opened her eyes. She looked past Marleena's bleached blond hair. And then she waited, keeping her eyes fixed there.

The candles flickering in the room caused the shadows of the two women to slowly dance across the wall. Leticia waited a little longer, but nothing remotely resembling Jesus popped up anywhere around.

Leticia studied her friend, her eyes closed, her lips mumbling in prayer. She noticed that Marleena's fingers weren't shaking as they had been. Then Leticia thought about miracles and how belief could maybe make almost anything occur. And though she didn't see Jesus standing there, she went ahead and said, "Oh, my goodness. I see him. He's here."

Padre Raimundo's Army

Arthur Powers

(Northern Goiás - Brazil, 1931 - 1975)

The countryside was not really dangerous. Yet, for a seven-year-old boy, walking alone the long *legua* to school, the stories came back – jaguars and anacondas, red guará wolves and wolfmen – though these last were supposed to come out only at night. Gunmen, bandits, witches, evil spirits . . . all the inhabitants of the stories told by old people around the fire on starlit nights.

Of course the boy knew – this from the stories too – that the good spirits were always stronger in the end. But usually an awful lot of terrible stuff happened before the good spirits prevailed.

There was one place, especially, on the path to school that he approached with fear – a long, shaded trail made by human and horse's feet through a stretch of rain forest. It was lovely and cool, but here – old Dona Ursula said – a goblin had rushed out one night and grabbed a thoughtless boy who had disrespected his elders – a boy never seen again.

"Hush, Ursula," Raimundo's mother said "– you're scaring the children." But old Ursula only grinned her toothless grin and winked at Raimundo in a way that made the story more frightening.

As he drew near this place on the path, Raimundo remembered that his Godmother had told him he had a guardian angel who always walked beside him. He found some comfort in this – then felt that, if one guardian angel was good company, additional saints and angels would be all the better. Going through his mind he remembered St. Anthony and the Angel Gabriel, St. Ann and the black Virgin of Aparecida, his dead uncle João – who everyone said was a saint. So that, by the time he reached the darkest twist in the path, he was a member of a lively, friendly group, filled with protective figures.

~

Raimundo excelled in the one-room, rural school – where good behavior and copying in neat handwriting were the essential skills for thriving. He finished all four grades, and when the priest came by for his twice-yearly visit, the schoolteacher brought the boy to his attention. The priest talked to the boy and, six months later, Raimundo went off to the minor seminary in a distant town, far from everything he had ever known.

He was a thin, thoughtful, timid boy, neither popular nor unpopular, not athletic or scholarly, a good student but not brilliant. He made his way through minor seminary and seminary adequately, without distinction, growing into a thin, thoughtful, somewhat timid man. Following ordination, he served as curate for two years in one of the villages in his native diocese, then was named pastor of a small church. He served as pastor in three parishes before coming to his last parish, Santa Maria das Aguas, in 1972. He was then forty-eight.

At Santa Maria das Aguas, as in his other parishes, the people developed a quiet fondness for Padre Raimundo. He was affable in his shy, retiring way – ready to listen, gentle in remonstrance, understanding in the confessional. When posed a particularly knotty question, he had a habit of saying, "I'll have to take that to counsel." Counsel with whom the people never thought to ask – there were no telephones in town in those days – but Padre Raimundo always seemed to come back later with a satisfactory – sometimes even profound – answer.

~

The bishop, of course, knew – in a way. Coming through

town one day unexpectedly, returning from another parish – he decided to drop by the rectory. The parish cleaning lady opened the door and the bishop, who had known Raimundo since seminary, asked for him. The cleaning lady nodded to the office door and said she thought the padre was in a meeting. Pausing at the door, the bishop heard Padre Raimundo's voice, but when the bishop peeked his head into the room, Padre Raimundo was alone, seated at his desk, with three empty chairs in a semicircle in front of him.

Padre Raimundo stood up. A smile of joy crossed his face as he saw the bishop.

"Am I interrupting anything?" the bishop asked.

"Not at all. We were just conferring."

"Conferring?"

"Yes. Whenever there's a problem, I find it helpful to confer with the saints. Just now, I was discussing the issue of a pregnant girl – no husband – with St. Teresa, St. Francis, and St. Thomas More. Have a seat."

The bishop glanced at the chair, hesitant to sit inadvertently on St. Thomas More's lap.

"Oh, it's all right," Padre Raimundo said. "We'd finished and they've gone."

The bishop sat. "Was the conference useful?" he asked.

"Very," Padre Raimundo answered. "Francis – well, I'm afraid Francis isn't really very helpful on *practical* matters – Teresa is always calling him to task on that. Thomas More is, of course, very practical in a *practical* way, if you know what I mean. But for these human questions – and aren't they mostly that? – Teresa's the one: she's a brick – solid, sensible, human – she always helps."

The bishop nodded. He knew the loneliness of these small towns, where each priest lived alone with a flock in which the educated could be counted on the fingers of one hand. He had himself often called upon spiritual help for counsel.

"I find the Archangel Michael helpful when I pray," said the bishop.

"Oh, definitely." Padre Raimundo nodded sagely. "But generally, I find saints are best for counsel, angels for action."

~

Despite his timid exterior, Padre Raimundo sometimes surprised his parishioners – at least those who did not know him well. When the Moraes family cornered the three Lamas brothers in an adobe hut at the edge of town and were going to kill them – Zeca Lamas had knifed a Moraes nephew in a drunken brawl the night before – Padre Raimundo walked quietly into the middle of the gunfight, argued the Moraes into common sense, persuaded Zeca to give himself up to the state police, and waited with him until the police arrived some six hours later. When Dona Elsa Guimarães, the largest and most feared landowner in the area, evicted a tenant farmer, his wife, and six children from their farm because she didn't like his politics, Padre Raimundo walked the five miles out to her plantation house and talked her into relenting – not pleading, people said, but remonstrating hard and strong.

Yet he was completely unprepared for the *grileiros* when they came into the area. The *grileiros* were not local strongmen, acting out of anger or revenge, although they got a few of the local riff-raff to work for them. They were professionals, backed by big money and expert at getting people off the land. Most of the small and middle-sized farmers – and even some of the larger landholders – didn't have legal titles. They had, in some cases, been on the land for generations, and so had legal rights – but almost none of them knew this.

The *grileiros'* methods were simple. They would find an area of small landholders. Smooth agents would go into the area and tell the people that they – the agents – represented the real owners of the land. They would have a paper purporting to prove this. They would tell the farmers that they – the farmers – had no rights, but that the owners, being generous, would pay them an indemnification for the land and would move them into town. In the early days, half the families would fall for this – living on the land was hard, the indemnification looked like a lot of money (they had never had to buy food or pay rent), life in town seemed better. They signed papers, received a handful of cash, and were dumped by the trucks at the edge of town, where a small slum started to grow.

The families who didn't agree were approached again. They were on the land illegally, they were told. Veiled threats were made. Crops were burned, pigs slaughtered in the night. More families gave in. Those who did not were increasingly isolated. Houses were burned. A farmer was killed, then another. In the end, only the very brave remained.

Within a few years, the Church would establish a network of lawyers and field workers to fight the *grileiros*. But at this time, nobody quite knew what was going on. Individual bishops and priests spoke out against the *grileiros*, who retorted that priests were trouble-makers, communists, should attend to their prayers and leave the business of land alone.

Padre Raimundo knew almost nothing of these controversies. But, talking to the families slowly starving in the little slum, he was appalled. His first thought was to get them food. But then? He went to a neighboring town to see the state judge. The judge, whom he had known for years, took him quietly into his study and, sweating, told him that he – the judge – couldn't do anything. He was afraid for himself and for his family. The state policemen Padre Raimundo had known were transferred out of the area – the new police simply looked at him and laughed.

This was the situation the day that Zé Severino was arrested.

~

Zé Severino was the leader of a group of small landholders who had resisted. Pascano, a tough, wiry little thug who worked for the *grileiros*, complained to the police that Zé Severino was threatening his life – Zé Severino had told Pascano to get off his land. Pascano and three policemen went out to Zé Severino's homestead. He heard the jeep coming, picked up his old hunting musket, and came outside – his wife and five kids behind him. They arrested him for armed resistance, brought him back into town, and threw him in jail. For an hour neighbors heard yelling, groans, and the sound of beating in the jail. Someone ran to tell Padre Raimundo.

Word ran all around town – as it does in small towns – that Padre Raimundo was coming. It was after 11 a.m. – the sun was hot and the dusty street nearly empty, but a shiver seemed to run along it.

The jail stood on a small rise, at the end of the street where it forked into two roads that wandered out into the country. It was a small, squat, insignificant building. Two of the police had left a few minutes before, driving in the ramshackle Volkswagen police car down to the *pensão* to eat lunch. So there were only three men watching the jail, and they were standing out in front where a big mango tree cast rich shade: Pascano, a tall consumptive police clerk named Elias, and Corporal Oliveira – one of the police who had arrested Zé Severino, and the most active in beating him – a hard-muscled, thick-headed mountain of a man. All three were armed. They had been drinking *cachaça* – handing the bottle back and forth – or even they might not have done what they did.

"Here comes the word of God," Pascano remarked wryly, and the other two turned to see Padre Raimundo walking alone up the street. Something in the priest's manner – the thin, unimpressive figure marching as though he were at the head of an army – struck Pascano funny, and he laughed. "Let's see how brave he is," Pascano muttered. He pulled out his revolver, aimed a little above the priest's head, and fired. Padre Raimundo continued walking without faltering. Pascano's amusement turned to irritation. "The damn interfering fool," he said, and fired another bullet close to the priest's feet. Padre Raimundo came on without a pause. Then Corporal Oliveira raised his pistol, fired, and – through fool luck or destiny – sent a bullet into Padre Raimundo's heart.

Dona Aparecida, an elderly widow, who was looking out her window near the jail, says that – as he fell – Padre Raimundo raised his arm in a motion like that of a commander waving his troops forward. Old Seu Geraldo, who lives across the street, confirms what she says. These are the only witnesses who have admitted seeing anything – their eyesight is good and their sincerity unquestionable, but of course both are very old.

They say that, as he fell, motioning with his arm, it was as if a great wind swept up the hill toward the jail – though there was no wind, they admit that. The leaves on the mango tree remained still. But there was a rush – not a sound, really, nor really a light – but a rush up towards the jail. Pascano began to shout, as if half in anger, half in fear, and fired his revolver twice before being spun around helpless, his arms pinned to his side. Corporal Oliveira yelled and ran forward, as if counter-attacking, before falling unconscious to the ground. Elias simply threw up his two arms in a cross to cover his face, and fell in terror to his knees. The wind – or whatever it was – rushed past him and into the jail house, bursting open the cell room door, and a stunned Zé Severino walked out of jail, free.

~

The official report, prepared by an intelligent, enlightened police major from the state capital, concluded that the people in town had risen up and stormed the prison, releasing the prisoner. No one was located who would admit to having seen anything except for two old people who told an impossible tale of wind and light. The major criticized the close ties between the police in rural areas and *grileiros,* noting that it undercut the credibility of law enforcement, and urged reform.

No witnesses except two old people. Corporal Oliveira, after he gained consciousness, sat – a huge broken lump of mountain – and looked up into people's eyes; "I'm sorry," he would say to them about nothing in particular, "I'm sorry."

This lasted a few months and then he vanished – nobody knows where. Pascano was committed to a hospital in the state capital; in between periods when he seemed normal and remembered nothing of the incident, he would have panic attacks, clinging to the medical assistants and screaming – "Don't let them – they're coming." In one of these attacks he shouted, "their golden swords!" Elias said nothing at all for six months; resigning from the police, he went to work as a cook for the Franciscans, spending his free hours helping the poor. His consumption had healed.

But these were all psychological ephemera. No doubt the official report was correct – it was very intelligently written.

Yet the bishop, driving home after praying at Padre Raimundo's funeral, kept remembering: "Saints are for counsel, angels for action."

Frank Russo

In the Museum of Creation

In the beginning is a dark room, a fiery ball
projected on a screen, its edges blurred, flickering.
A soundscape of hissing, gurgling
makes way for starburst synthesizers
as a voice speaks of the fallacies of learning
and of knowing. The ceiling
is pricked with the tiny lights
of celestial bodies, a papier-mâché moon,
planets daubed with acrylics
suspended from strings.
One hundred and forty-eight days
it took to complete this room—one hundred and forty-seven
more than the creator.

I'd lost my way at the turnoff to Tierrasanta, drifted
on the road to Idlewild, until I came across a sign
outside Abilene, which said the Life of Christ
performed Fridays and Saturdays.
A drive-through attendant pointed in the direction
of the dinosaur fields, where the fossil of a human finger
from a girl's left hand
was found in Cretaceous earth.
In the distance was the structure,
fashioned from concrete, glass and steel.

In a vine-covered room Pterodactyl bones hang
from a cathedral canopy. Trunks of prehistoric
firs, fat as water-soaked boabs, rise from a bog garden
adorned with Venus flytrap and pitcher plant.
A frog, speckled red, clings to a leaf. A snake—

too measured in its movements to have tempted Eve—
coils behind glass. Giant Morphos
are pinned beside Swallowtails and Common Jezebel,
wings orange-tipped like painted fingernails. The recorded
                                          calls of birds
and gibbon shrieks echo from speakers fastened to a metal
                                              palm.

A stream too small for Pishon or Gihon
cascades over fiberglass rocks. Waist-high,
Adam rises from a pool, Eve beside him—black hair
covering her breasts, as though she already knows shame;
their faces amalgams of every tribe, melting pots from which
the races of the world might disentangle.

In a room filled with monitors, the six days of creation
are screened on repeat in four minute segments.
At a touch Noah appears in wheat-colored cloth.
With a California accent he explains how the alligator
and Komodo dragon were the only dinosaurs
to come aboard the Ark with his family of eight.
Press 'Back' and a monochromatic screen flashes green,
offering the option of meeting Jesus, Moses or Abraham.

In the gardens grow trees from each continent,
allowing visitors to savor Eden.
At the far end is a petting zoo, where a zonkey and a zorse are
                                          exhibited.
A child watches in awe, asks what each creature is.
"They were bred that way to create something new,
as God had done," her mother explains.
The child can't find the words to ask
why man would make such animals, to display,
as if fifteen thousand kinds of butterfly
and four hundred thousand varieties of beetle weren't
                                          enough—

leaving Darwin to discover sixty-nine in one day, and
ornithologists and entomologists years to categorize and
bring order to the products of creation.

Nativity of Christ Cathedral, Riga

The light flooding through the windows illuminates
gilded panels of icons, making it hard to believe
this could ever have been converted to a place of Lutheran
                                                  worship
or a planetarium—icons removed,
gigantic bells melted to bullion.
Beneath the candelabra brightly head-scarfed women
and men in ushanka hats line up
to touch the glass-sided casket containing an Orthodox saint,
its corners bejeweled with winged angels,
as though it might lift Heavenwards. The outline
of the saint's corpse is visible beneath an embroidered sheet;
                                                  his face
covered with a black velvet mask.
A red velvet cap sits atop what might be a bare cranium
or leathered skin, half-embalmed,
too holy or gruesome to expose;
the perfume of incense overpowering.

Blind Faith

Reading the tale of Jairus' daughter, brought back from the
dead,
of Bartimaeus, whose sight was restored,
of Peter's mother-in-law, her fever lifted,
and of Mob, from whom a demon was cast,
his eyelids became heavy,
the pages from his King James Bible
falling to his side, as they did each night; the Xalatan
untouched in his medicine cabinet.

Reading of the lame, the dumb, the crippled—all of them
healed—
until he could no longer tell a C from a D
or a q from a p on his eye-doctor's wall chart;
reading until the drops prescribed for him
could no longer work any miracles.

Good Friday, Lake Victoria

Sixteen set off from the shore of the lake
in a boat christened Salvation, singing
prayers and hymns, accompanied by tambourines

and organ. The engine cut as their chants
became a fever, as one by one they stepped
forward, as Christ the fisherman had, to glide

across the water. Could those who stepped out last

see those who had gone before them? Did they
see them skate across the surface like Jesus birds?

Their bodies lighter than water. Chanting
as they watched each person move closer
to the heart of the inland sea, stepping off,
one by one, into the cool silent water.

The Caves of Atapuerca

Imagine the awe of the cave climbers
as they move the rockfall to expose
the entrance to the *Galeria del Silex*—
the Flint Gallery: the hush, the mist
of vapor on the walls, torches revealing
zigzags, appendages, grids, a string
of dots in red and black. The image
of a man with hands raised; another holding
a bow. Their eyes adjusting to the dark,
resting on the panel of the sun, its rays
carved into rock, their torches shining
on something resembling the fletching of an arrow—
a climber, realizing this as a place of sun-worship,
makes out the outline of an ear of grain.

At the entrance to *El Portalon* of the *Cueva Maya*,
a painting depicts a horse's head, but the oxide
deteriorates too quickly for it to be genuine—
painted instead by a local, intent on fame
or deceit or stirred by a yearning so innate
to reproduce what lies deep within his DNA.

This cave like Rome, lived in for centuries—
in the Bronze Age by hunters and grazers
who left behind fragments of bowl, ceramics
etched with teeth, necklaces fashioned from horn and bone.
Beneath these middens paleontologists
exhume the frames of deer, birds, wild boar
mixed with nettle seeds and earth.
Our guide explains how in the *Gran Dolina* cave,
the etchings found on human and animal bones
are suggestive of cannibalism.
"They make up such bullshit out of nothing," says the man
                                             from Almeria,
pointing to a rock the size and color of a melon, its existence
here in this case being proof of ancient pizza ovens.

A five-hundred meter crawl, then a chimney drop
to the *Sima de los Huesos*—the pit of bones—
cut like a gash by the railway cutting,
the cave floor once covered in debris and sediment,
hiding bones of lynxes, foxes, wildcats,
an *Ursus deningeri*, and further still, human bones—
mandibles, femurs, vertebrae,
ribs of *Homo heidelbergensis*, the remains
of a pelvis five-hundred thousand years old,
christened Elvis. In 92 a complete cranium—
this they called Miguelon, as if he were a local farmer
dug up from the *Cementerio Municipal*.
His jawbone they found the following summer.
But none mattered as much as what they found
amongst fragments of bone and debris—a chunk of pink
                                                      quartz,
tossed into the pit as an offering, a symbol—
perhaps the oldest known to humankind?

Half a day by foot rises the cathedral of Burgos, light filtering

through the stonework tracery on its octagonal towers.
In the Chapel *de las reliquias* an altarpiece contains
amputated fingers, the remains of a female saint
in a crystal urn, five fragments from the Holy Cross,
a thorn from Jesus' crown.
The sound of camera shutters and footsteps
over the marble tombs of bishops and mercenaries
is met by whispers from attendants,
their petitions of *No flash, No flash*
rising like a hum.

The glory of the One who moves all things penetrates all the universe, reflecting in one part more and in another less.

Dante Alighieri

Zipora

Rivka Keren

Translated from Hebrew by Yael Politis

The last days of summer, noon of a scorching day. Two young girls slither through the break in the wall that separates the PAGI neighborhood from no man's land and gaze at the rocky terrain, the garbage, the rusty signs and at the one stain of bright color which is a glimpse of Zipora's dress as she leans on Beno Gottzeit's arm within the cloak of secrecy the couple has imagined for themselves while everyone else is fast asleep.

Edna and Sarah squeeze through the narrow opening, one watching her father, the other her mother, a sight so cruelly fascinating that no fear or danger can distract their attention from it. Right here, in this corner, they had also found that pamphlet with its mass of naked images, contorted in unspeakable suffering. *Hieronymus* something-or-other had been the name of the artist, and ever since then, whenever they wanted to give one another a hint in a secret language they would say *Hieronymus*, and that is what Edna says now, *Hieronymus*, and Sarah reiterates it like a password, and they run home in their long stockings, dripping with sweat, breathless, what could they do now that everyone knew, and how wouldn't they know, in this place where everybody knows who has hemorrhoids, who took up the hem of her dress, and who was lazy and skipped evening prayers. Daughters of sinners they call them, and pelt them with pine cones and gravel, and the circle of attackers constantly grows. Well, pious Jews, we now know beyond all doubt that Benjamin Gottzeit has forsaken his newly wedded wife who was betrothed to him after he barely escaped from Europe and is openly committing adultery with the wife of a scholar, that sums up the whole affair, and the two families, indeed, live next door to one another, have adjacent porches, and the voices pass through the walls creating a sweet and lethal closeness that ripens in the very heart of the angry community.

Strips of sunlight across the bed, the sound of running water, the smell of cooking cabbage. The two girls shut themselves up in their rooms, braiding one another's hair, studying pictures taken out from behind holy books, a dark pact of prolonged lechery binds them. Your father seduced my mother; Your mother seduced my father. Is this thing that arouses in them such excitement and loathing called love, and is love a painful inclination that besets the curious? They talk this subject over and go out again, crossing the courtyard surrounded by balconies and the paved entry under the synagogue domes, going farther away, down the steep slope toward the Sanhedria Park to gather the magical stones that are scattered at the mouths of the burial caves and equipped with seven of these transparent stones they head toward the last cave, the one that has seventy one niches carved into the rock. The park is empty and laced with shadows, and opposite, above the crest of hills, rises David's Tower, blurred and unattainable, just as Edna will see it one day years later, when she will return here with Zohar.

Sarah sits on the floor of the cave arranging the stones in a circle, picks up a piece of chalk and says, Say the words one by one, a word for each stone, like we decided, and Edna stands facing the niches and says, *Fire, love, lightening, hell, penitence, earth, water*. Sarah writes the words on the floor, a word for each stone, and says Mother seven times, then it's Edna's turn to murmur Father seven times, and they remain there at length in the moldy silence, while outside daylight falls in blinding sheathes and is trapped in the treetops, and Sarah gathers up the stones and buries them at the entry to the cave, and uses the soles of her shoes to rub out the words, saying,

We've done everything we should, now all we can do is wait for an answer.

Towards evening the heat wave breaks under the force of a westerly wind. Zipora polishes the silver candlesticks for the holidays with soft motions, polishes and hums to herself, and the lamplight forms a halo about her face. Sarah puts her brothers to bed, washes the dishes, then rests her head on the palms of her hands and watches her mother, her forehead, eyes, nose, mouth. She will shortly rise and go out to the stairwell to meet Benjamin Gottzeit to wish him a good night, and Edna will also be standing there behind her father, pale and barefoot, her hair mussed, and she will signal her friend, *Hieronymus*, heh? And the doors will close, but not for long. At two in the morning Zipora will cautiously open the door and let herself into Beno's apartment remaining there for a long time, and while Sarah lays on her bed paralyzed with fear lest her father awake, Edna presses up against the partition in the middle of the room, not a sound, the lovers must have turned to stone, and then Zipora comes back to slip between the sheets at her husband's side, and the two little girls, separated by only a thin wall, feel a pressing distress, Here, the words of the incantation have set off on their long journey, carrying with them all possibilities.

These nights are laden with the odor of dust and withering and the wild dogs from Jordan pass through the courtyards of the neighborhood like a storm, devouring cats. Whoever is awake at that hour cannot but hear the chorus of barks, wails of despair, and the sound of iron shutters creaking on their hinges and banging in the wind. And those who sleep probably dream of the judgment day. One morning the first drops of rain fall.

It's a good sign, the little girls think to themselves.

They hurry down Shmuel Hanavi Street towards the Mandelbaum Gate, skipping in and out of the cement cones positioned in the road as tank barriers, and they soon turn off the paved road into an abandoned field that is sectioned off by barbed wire and in which stands a ruin, scattered with bullet casings and rusty grenade pins, and Sarah says, If they see us they'll shoot us, and they bend down, dragging their school bags on the ground, and Edna thinks, *Fire, love, lightening, hell, penitence, earth, water,* saying, I wrote a letter to my father. They go into their hiding place and Sarah takes the page in her hand, asking, What is this? and Edna replies, Hungarian.

"Drága apukám könyörgöm ne találkozz a cipórával mert bántani fognak nagyon szeretlek téged," It's easier for him to understand Hungarian, Edna says, I wrote, "My dear Pappa, I am begging you not to see Zipora anymore because they will hurt you, I love you very much." Are you going to give it to him face to face? Sarah asks, and Edna puts the letter back into her schoolbag and replies, I'll give it to him and wait while he reads it and tells me what he thinks, and Sarah says, God help you; if I were you I'd be scared to death; how do you know Hungarian? and Edna smiles, saying, The nuns taught me during the war, and silently mouths the forbidden words of the prayer, sometimes from force of habit her hand still reaches towards her chest, and the cross isn't there, They are both prayers, so what's the difference, do the unacceptable prayers fall down from the skies and turn into bans and curses? and Sarah asks in a whisper, The nuns? and Edna doesn't reply but hugs her friend and they hear a bell ringing and a tapping sound and the shriek of the wind in the open fields. What would you wish for more than anything? Sarah asks, and Edna replies, I can't say, and Sarah says, I would wish that . . . and she draws a circle in the earth with her finger and wipes away a tear with her dirty hand, and the unfinished sentence hovers in the gap between hope and despair, I would wish that . . .

And this is the order of events: the girls visit the park every day to make sure that the magical stones are still well buried and the words of the incantation are completely erased, and then they sit in the park facing the rock swearing eternal loyalty to one another. Make believe that we are sisters, Sarah says, and Edna stares at the trees and says nothing. And while they are sitting in the park, watching the flight of the incantation in their thoughts, anonymous persons are breaking the windows in their apartments, slipping threatening letters into their mailboxes, and leaving crushed fish heads on their doorsteps. The members of the Morality Brigade secretly meet in the yeshivah building for a last deliberation. Zipora's husband beats his head against the wall and scrapes off bits of plaster like Beno Gottzeit had once done, alternately laughing and crying and cursing his neighbor, the son of a bitch, and the rabbi appointed to sit in judgment on the matter stands over him trying to calm him, saying, Shh, rest assured, he'll get what's coming to him, he'll spend the rest of his days in fear, as the trees of the forest are moved with the wind.

The synagogue is completely filled and the nearness of the holidays stirs hearts, this is not the place where penitential prayers and fasting will atone for the carryings-on of the lechers, and on one of the intermediate days of Succot, at midnight, they come for Beno, make a tear in his shirt, spit in his face, place him under ban and exile, while at the same time a group of strapping women drag Zipora down to the shelter in the basement of the building, rip the covering from her head, smear her short hair with glue, Whore, slut, woe to the eyes that behold you!

It's all over within two days. The scent of the flowering carob accompanies them on their long way, even after they have left behind the crowded stone building, and the Yemenite cart driver for the Machanaim neighborhood who is helping them to move their belongings, tied up in sheets, into their tiny one-room apartment, facing the cemetery, sighs and strokes his curly beard and thinks to himself, Just look at them. *Wallah*, an old man and a little girl all alone, what will they do here with the dead at night?

Since people's feelings of animosity have been satisfied and turned into smug pity, the news of Zipora's sudden death is kept from Benjamin Gottzeit, and he keeps on repeating to his daughter with yearning eyes, She went to America. And that's how he will continue to think of her all through the years, walking along in her muslin clothes between those tall buildings over there across the ocean, and even after someone breaks the bitter news to him, for indeed, that is what will happen in time, he will refuse to believe it, and will shake his head from side to side, *Nem, nem*, it's a filthy lie, I have borne my punishment. That kind of thing doesn't happen twice to a person.

Hilde's Son, the Rabbi

Michele Merens

Once Ezra was safely in the bathroom, he slapped water
from the sink onto his cheeks, then pulled one of Hilde's
towels off its brass ring. He relied on this embrace of water
and cotton to give him strength. These surrogates were all he
had, with the mirror covered and his reflection denied.

All the mirrors in the apartment were covered now, but not
with Hilde's special lavenders. Sarah had found half-a-dozen
white towels in her closets and decided they would be more
than adequate for the Jewish mourning ritual during the family
visitations. Never mind that his mother would've hardly
appreciated this pedestrian transformation of her bath, a
denial of one's reflection in the glass even as gleaming
perfumes lined up on the counter invited the opposite; that
strangers snare every scent they could, before selecting one to
distract or disarm.

No, it was hardly a sin to acknowledge – even on this day
of her burial – that Hilde had been a vain, extravagant woman
all her life. And while Ezra had never thought of himself as
having a large ego, maybe here in the privacy of Hilde's
bathroom, he could admit to feeling not much different than
she ever had. He had a brief, powerful urge to lift the towel
for a glimpse. How did he look right now, for instance? Was
his hair already beginning to shade with gray? He was only in
his fifties, but he'd seen enough people in his congregation
turn almost completely after their second parent passed.

His fingers moved forward to caress the towel's cotton
fringe. Then God made a gentle joke. What of the tallis, Ezra,
that fringe? Vaguely, he could still smell Hilde's brand of soap
on the towel, acting as a lure, but no. Of course, he wouldn't
cheat. He was a rabbi because the rules of his religion gave

comfort, not privilege. Customs simply weren't to be questioned simply because they were inconvenient; he wouldn't lift the towel off the mirror to see how he measured up, after all.

He released the towel, reminded himself that even a few seconds of distraction would undoubtedly add to the shameful feelings he suffered. That he was falling so far back into the role of her confused, obedient son too much this week, and not the competent rabbi he and so many others knew him to be. Today, he found himself falling apart in every conceivable test, regressing into a kind of hopeless paralysis of soul and logic, incapable of fighting off Hilde's old craziness at every turn – even now. And yet why? God help him. She had died, died! Yet had she come back from death so quickly to torture her son the rabbi with her contradictions, to make sure her wishes were, in the end, not to be denied?

"Our sympathies, rabbi."

"Thank you."

"She was a lovely woman."

"Wasn't she?"

"And she raised such fine boys, she was so proud of you both. A rabbi and a lawyer."

"Yes, I know. Thank you so much."

Rabbi, rabbi, rabbi. Not one of them knew him well enough to call him anything but, he'd been away too long. Yet standing at the foot of the bimah before the ceremony, he yearned for someone to address him by his real name. Now that Hilde was gone, there would be one less person on earth with the capacity to recognize him even from behind, call him first and always, Ezra. A tragedy few could empathize with, but who was left?

Sarah, of course. But right now when he was trying to communicate how much he needed her, she was separated from Ezra by at least three other people in the receiving line. Ezra tried to will her to exchange a glance, but – no. She knew the part she had to play at these times. Since they'd first met in Haifa and after so many decades of being his wife, she had trained herself to stand alert, pass a smile in response to every one of his remarks. And so again, here, she slipped almost transparently into her role of rabbi's helpmate, taking on every group of strangers as an instant congregation they would face together, and head on.

Still, after the funeral, he knew they would come together in their hotel room. That Sarah would take his hand up in hers, come close so that he could take in her breath, smell papaya-sweet. In a few hours. He just needed to be patient.

For now, organ music and Rabbi Schering's appearance on the bimah acted as signals for the mourners to take their seats. Ezra embraced his brother, felt the scratch of his woolen suit against his chin.

"Take a breath," he whispered. His brother nodded, but sweat lined his forehead.

"You'll do fine," Ezra assured him before taking Sarah's hand and leading her to their seats in the first pew.

Perhaps it did take a few minutes for others to register what had occurred. Ezra kept his eyes focused on the podium, careful not to stray and fall into the net of anyone's censoring gaze. Yes, he was the rabbi, that son, but no. He would not be the one to eulogize his mother today.

They had decided in a short meeting in Rabbi Schering's oak-trimmed study. After all, Barry was a lawyer, just as eloquent with his words. The younger son, yes, but hadn't he always deferred to the firstborn? "Now it's Barry's turn," Ezra insisted. If he'd had any qualms, his brother's thoroughly grateful expression had calmed them.

So he'd been generous, even if his abdication was grounded in half-truths. For Ezra knew he couldn't play that role today, a rabbi whose words were hinged to measured, comforting tones. He understood he couldn't trust this voice, that constant mumbling in his ear, "You a rabbi? But today, you have nothing to say."

Fifty-three and he'd never felt this way in his life before, so completely mute with sorrow, so lodged in blackness lacking even a shadow. He hadn't even felt this weak at seven years old, when their father had died. Then, he'd held the sorrow close up near his heart under his coat at the burial site, feeling it had in some way a shape, a warmth to it, like a small, furry creature providing him with immeasurable comfort. He thought later that he'd found God when his father died, in that tiny beating warmth under his coat; that God's voice could be that close if one just looked for it, always.

But this grief was so different. This grief acted the thief and made off with the hopeful murmurs of the heart. Stole them right out from under his clothes, his very skin.

Stole his voice too, made this fraud of a rabbi practically mute. Why in the shower this morning he'd nearly slipped on the soap and lost his footing. The next moment had sparked terror as a picture came up in his head of falling against tiles, bleeding until he lost consciousness. And who would come in to investigate, who would even care? Yet he couldn't summon up a scream for help. His voice had been locked up low near his heart for some reason, so far from his throat. It took finding the shower bar and three long breaths, remembering Sarah in the other room, to recover.

As Barry took his place on the bimah, Ezra gave him all his attention. Do well, he silently urged his pug-faced brother. Barry looked up and tried to smile. Because of the usual bloat of his cheeks, the goodwill appeared pained.

"Many of you know Hilde because of her passions," he began, his voice steady but low. "You knew her as someone willing to argue with family or friends or strangers on the street if she believed in a cause. But most of you probably didn't mind, because Hilde could argue her case with a good punch line as often as not."

To this remark, the crowd chuckled politely.

"As you know, she was an émigré to our country from France. All her life, Hilde had wonderful French sensibilities. But she was also Jewish and identified herself in that way. She was a survivor of World War II, along with being a wife and mother and American."

Ezra cocked his head, snapping to attention. Why was his brother talking about Hilde as a French Jew? They both knew so well of their mother's hostility to conventional religiosity yet this was his interpretation? Hilde would've laughed outright.

No, please, Barry, don't talk about how she was a survivor of the War, don't go there.

Besides how could he know, what did he dare say? The war, and Judaism itself, was a subject Hilde spoke of as little as possible, and only when forced to by relatives, friends. She tolerated the fact that her husband observed, yet wondered at the mystery that one of her sons had ever joined the Rabbinate; for surely Ezra had to know her view on Judaism, hadn't she spelled it out years ago, hadn't he understood? *"Filthy Jews, that's what I heard all my life, how we all were filthy, filthy Jews. And of course we became what they said, herded in those camps. We couldn't be anything else but what they made us out to be. Well, that's it. I turn my back on all of it forever now. Filthy Jews. I never want to hear either of those words in my house again."*

But here he was, a rabbi nonetheless, and here was her other son, Barry, skipping over that part, misinterpreting, distorting. Not saying how she donated the Sabbath candlesticks to Goodwill the week after her husband died. Not mentioning how she begged off every bar mitzvah of nephews, took trips to Florida every Passover when the rest of the family gathered for Seders. When Ezra himself had confessed to a need to embrace Judaism as a lifelong vocation, she'd laughed outright in amazement. Just remember how, over one of her steaming brie brioches, she'd raised an eyebrow, anchored the knife in the air before slicing. "Why do you even want to? Be a rabbi of all things? Have people come, complain, ask you to fix their lives . . ."

"I thought you would be proud," he'd protested, startled more than anything else.

"Good luck to you then, Ezra, be a good Jew," she said, turning her eyes away to slice, going thin at the crust. "But don't come home so smug that you tell me to stop my bridge games on the Sabbath. Don't tell me to attend synagogue on Saturday mornings. I shop on Saturdays. Don't make me feel bad anymore, about who's a good Jew and who's not a good Jew in this life. No one gets to do that to me, anymore . . . ."

With great pain, Ezra had tried to reconcile his mother's views, not take it personally. Being called a filthy Jew, subjected to the horrors of wartime internment when young, had left her with the scars of a traumatized child, even into her old age. No one can blame the victim for trying to transform herself, no one.

Barry had to know this reality as well as Ezra ever did. Yet here he stood parading Hilde forth as an observant Jew. For all his brilliance as a lawyer, he obviously had never been sensitive to their mother's many contradictions on this topic. And yes his brother was embarrassing himself up on the bimah, not knowing what he spoke of in any meaningful way.

Yet he the rabbi had no right to criticize. He hadn't said a word to temper Barry's speech; he simply hadn't trusted his own instincts. For he knew in one unguarded moment he might spill the truth as he understood it and betray his mother's memory for good: *No Barry, you're wrong. Our mother wasn't pledged to Zionism, Israel, France, or America. Hilde's allegiance in her old age was always to Hilde, and Hilde alone.*

"Yisgadal, v'yiskadash, sh'mey rabbo . . ."

As the mourners rolled their tongues around Kaddish, Ezra found this traditional Jewish prayer for the dead a most welcome and familiar refrain. The sun at the gravesite was heavy on his back and yet another unexpected embrace in this season. An awning swung over four poles and set into muddy ground provided more cover; still, Sarah dug into her purse for sunglasses.

"Put the glasses away, please," Ezra wanted to say. He couldn't bear not being able to see his wife's brilliant, blue eyes when his mother was finally laid in the ground. But then Rabbi Schering started up the prayers and he could do no more than repeat the familiar chants, fill his mouth with words that felt as thick as bread on the tongue.

He shifted his gaze onto the silver-trimmed casket, the expensive, heavy box. But this sight, unlike the weather or the prayer for the dead, gave no comfort. Jewish tradition called for plain pine, the starkest choice. Yet Ezra had said nothing when the savvy funeral director leaned in so close to push for this model instead. He was the one who knew the Jewish laws, what rules were inviolate and which could be perhaps reinterpreted under Reform strictures, not Barry. Yet he'd stayed silent when his brother, eager to indulge their mother's love for the ornate even in death, instead chose the more expensive casket.

Any son of Hilde's listens to what Hilde wants, first and always.

So no matter as a rabbi, he knew better. No matter his love for Judaism coursed just as strong within, punishing him for these breaks with Jewish traditions. No matter that he had deferred to all these odd choices, not giving the eulogy, picking the pricey casket, rolled over on all his inclinations to suit his mother's will, not his own, in these final moments of sharing. His love for Hilde and his love for God wrapped up as one and the same, so there was no getting out, no breathing space; *honor your mother and father*, the first commandment, the most important certainly, today, and so how could any of it ever be untangled?

The anger, the blackness of those constant humiliations, came up through his gut, into his throat. Not expecting such strong feelings, Ezra gritted his teeth. Suddenly, he was terrified of what might fall out of him in front of these strangers, into her grave.

He took a short breath, tried to find his focus in the cloud of air that came with an exhalation. Instead, his head burned and with a shudder, the first tears. As he tried to wipe away the salty wetness on both cheeks with the back of one hand, more tears, then snot, spilled forth. He quickly went into his coat pocket for a tissue, intending to recover or hide.

His fingers tugged on a handkerchief. Sarah must've tucked one in there before the service. His glance went to her, *Thank you*. Yet he knew this one handkerchief wouldn't be enough. The scent of his cologne, like fresh tea, came up to distract him from other, more troublesome smells and thoughts: the dank soil, still moist from where shovels had turned up the earth; a slightly feral odor coming off of a woman's black fur coat.

"Y'hey sh'mey rabo m'vorach . . ."

At the conclusion they will say, May these words give peace to all who mourn and to all who mourn we say Amen.

To all who mourn, and yet. How could he mourn this woman in the traditional Jewish ways? When she wouldn't let him, had never let him.

He had uttered these same words of mourning prayer so many times before, in fast clouded breaths to get out of the bad weather, or slow and loud, to soothe slightly deaf relatives at funerals. But when he needed them, what did these words do? With what rhythm did he need to speak, to stop thinking of this hard bridge chair he sat on and instead consider that coffin, the sun beating on his own mother's grave?

And then there was mercifully, silence. Rabbi Schering turned a page in his prayer book then lifted his face to the mourners under the awning. With a nod, he beckoned them to rise.

It will soon be over, Ezra realized. Mama will be laid in the ground next to Papa. He's been waiting for her for a long time. He looked at the well-tended grave spots reserved for his own family nearby, and took his first peaceful breath of the day.

Then it was time, time for men to collapse the mount, pivot the casket into the hole. Ezra rose, then walked in tandem with Barry to the rough grass edging of the grave. He didn't want to watch any of the mechanics, but nonetheless could hear the steel legs of the stand shift and groan as the coffin was dropped into the ground.

Rabbi Schering's sleeve brushed up against Ezra's arm. He handed him the trowel, mouthed silently that he should begin. As Hilde's eldest son, he was expected to honor her in the Jewish custom by throwing the first heap of dirt onto her casket.

He moved his glance to the small pile of dirt left for mourners to scoop by the gravesite. He didn't remove his eyes from the pile, even as he became aware of others lining up behind him, coughing, crying, dragging their feet, to complete this holiest of rituals.

And of course, it was their honor to give this to Hilde. Laying a handful of dirt on a grave is the last thing the living can do for the dead, the last kind act any Jew can provide to another on this earth. It must be done.

Ezra fisted the trowel.

But this was Hilde. This was his fastidious mother, his mere. "A filthy Jew, a dirty Jew. I never want to hear either of those words in this house again."

She'd hate this, too.

No, no, he argued back to his own demons. Throwing dirt on the coffin was a Jew's highest honor to another, a way the living speak to the dead, a mitzvah. He couldn't let his own mother go unescorted into the grave, could he? He couldn't turn from this faith he dearly loved to once again please Hilde.

And at this last juncture, with God so close . . . did he even dare?

Ezra's shoulders suddenly seemed to push forward as if something besides mild air was coming up from behind. Yet he felt incapable of moving to protect himself. His feet also seemed not to be grounded where he stood at the lip of the grave. Looking at her coffin lodged in the ground, he felt mostly dizzy. And, something more, if he could only admit it.

Just who do you need to respect here, Ezra? Your mother or your God?

Ezra pulled his glance away from the heap of dirt, swiveled on a heel to view the line forming behind him. The other mourners didn't expect this move. Some raised eyebrows in confusion.

Sarah was staring too. He could see a bluish vein bulging on her neck, as it did when she was worried. Ah, Sarah. Even behind those glasses, he could glimpse how deep was her concern. He was so lucky to have her, all these many years of her. How many years had she helped him navigate familial standoffs with enduring patience. How she'd willingly took the heat off of both brothers at times with their intractable, impossible Mama. How this woman helped him live life, by always standing so near, no matter what.

Ezra gazed down at his mother's coffin, draped only in a prayer shawl. And he realized what to do to reconcile all that had never been, in his lifetime, and Hilde's too.

For his beautiful, vain, stubborn mother had been made to feel so filthy as a Jew all her life. Doused herself in perfumes and jewelry, cursed and moaned; yet she'd never found her way out of the dirt.

Today, at least, let her not feel that dirt, that weight against her, because of his mere need to love.

Rabbi Schering's prayers drifted up and into his ears. ". . . V'imroo omain."

"Ose sholom bimromov, hoo yaaseh sholom oleynoo v'al kol yisroel, v'imroo omain."

Ezra shook out his shoulders, let every part of his body relax under the suit. He motioned to Barry then handed him the trowel.

Barry moved over with a questioning glance.

"Not you first?"

"Not me, at all," he said.

He looked past his wife then and over to a man, a stranger in a beige overcoat who was whispering to a woman in the line. Ezra couldn't hear what was said with Barry mumbling into his handkerchief, making so much noise. But he could guess.

"The rabbi's broken down. He can't take it, the grief's too much."

Some others too, they were staring at the unrepentant rabbi as he stepped back from the grave, and what questions were in their head?

But Ezra didn't care. He wouldn't have cared if these people were part of his own congregation. The thought nearly brought on a smile, even more so when he realized that those feelings of fear and weakness which had tormented most of the day were slipping away. Instead, unexpected emotions were rising inside. And what were they exactly? Surprising – a sense of giddiness, an urge to laugh out loud.

Any kind of laugh or smile wouldn't be appropriate though, he reminded himself. That wouldn't be behavior fitting any son, any mourner, much less a rabbi at a gravesite. Who among those watching would begin to understand such irreverence?

With the most sober nod he could offer them instead, Ezra turned from his mother's grave and simply, silently, walked to his chair.

Whoever you are holding me now in hand,
Without one thing all will be useless,
I give you fair warning before you attempt me further,
I am not what you supposed, but far different.

Walt Whitman

One Traveler

Julie J. Nichols

Just before he left for his mission, Jacob crunched Sammy's shoulders in the folds of his arms. "You can do this," he whispered. "You have to. Remember, I'll be doing it too. Just farther away."

"Doing what?"

"Choosing the right," he said, softly, fiercely. She knew what he meant. With Jacob she felt grown-up, smart, discussing things into the night, after their parents went to bed. "Choose the right." It was a song in the hymnbook, one of many they'd punned upon, even before they moved here three years ago so their mother could help out after their grandpa's stroke, this place so unlike the city they'd been born in, with its museums and cathedrals, its monuments and parks. Choose the write? Choose right-wing, fundamentalist politics? More seriously, they debated *what* was "right." Goodness? Truth? And if only certain behaviors or concepts were right, what about what was *left*?

So when he said that, it was code for "don't despair, no matter what." And that kept her from wailing, when he left on his mission, and every day since. He and he alone would have understood how she felt at this exact moment, the night before Christmas, stuck in the caboose of the Callahans' Christmas train with baby Mariel Hartsough, daughter of Mr. Harry H. Hartsough, principal and (worse) eighth-grade Life Sciences teacher at Pine Valley K-8. Mr. H was wrong, wrong, wrong about Life, and Sammy knew it, and Jacob would have known it too. Mr. Stupid H had foisted his nursling daughter, baby Mariel, on her to get back at her, to force her to answer his test questions his way. If she took care of Mariel on the all-school field trip through the Callahans' Christmas show, he told her, so that he could stay behind and get some last-minute work done, then Sammy could make up points on that last disastrous exam.

Sammy suspected that this was highly unethical. What she'd put on the test wasn't wrong. If Jacob were here, he'd know what to do. In her next email she'd tell him. He'd be proud of her clarity, sympathetic to her plight. Meanwhile, she sat apart from the rest of the school kids, hating Mr. H, hating Mariel, hating Christmas, this first Christmas without Jacob, her capital-e Elder brother, nineteen and on a two-year mission in Colombia, South America for the Mormon Church.

That she hated more than anything. She *needed* him. Here, people said "crick" for "creek" (there were actually creeks), and sometimes "we ain't" or "we was." Here, winter, spring, summer, fall, the big entertainment was this one-eighth-size railroad, an engine with three open passenger cars and this tiny caboose, rattling along in the Callahan family compound on a snaking track five miles from start to finish, inhabited, from season to season, via an agreement with local schools, by scores of children joggling on the benches, observing orchards in spring bloom, cornfields hung about with summer scarecrows, a turkey farm in full operation in autumn, hot buttered half-cobs at the end. In August, toddlers and their mothers relaxed in the sun for fifteen minutes of "sprinkle-train." Because everybody did all this – everybody! – Sammy and Jacob had done it all too, mocking behind their hands the whole time, keeping it between themselves, a conspiracy of not belonging.

At Christmas, the Callahans outdid themselves. Regardless of subzero temperatures, icy roads, cutting winds, even, like tonight, threatening blizzards, down-bundled comers of all ages huddled together for the red-and-green spotlit ride through Santa Claus Land. Lollipop elves with big red ribbons made an army on one side, child-sized candy canes and bow-festooned Christmas trees a forest on the other till the halfway point, and then came the second part, the part about "the real meaning of Christmas." The schools all made it a last-week-before-vacation excursion. Mr. Hartsough offered it to the whole K-8, assuming – so wrongly – that everybody was thrilled. *Some* people had other things to do. Even if they wouldn't say so out loud, because they felt they *had* to go, and pretend they liked it, babysitting the principal's five-year-old the entire time, in order to pass Life Sciences 8.

Now the last car juddered down the tracks behind the rest, unsettling Sammy's vertebrae, jostling toward the station house where they would disembark to visit Santa. Lines from a poem Mr. Severs read aloud just yesterday in English class drifted up through Sammy's anger into her better mind: *A cold coming we had of it, / Just the worst time of the year / For a journey, and such a long journey . . .*

Yes, yes, it was.

Baby Mariel slid down the slat bench of the caboose, tugging at the drawstrings of her jacket's hood, complaining about the cold. Four or five clots of snow spat from the darkening cumulus. Sammy reached over to pull the nylon cords from Mariel's fingers and tied a fierce knot. "What's the matter with you?" she muttered. Well, she knew: the child's mom was preoccupied with three other babies littler than Mariel, and her dad was Mr. Hartsough. Sammy would whimper too if that were her lot. "Never mind," Sammy said. "Go to sleep or something." Mariel looked away.

Mr. Severs was the only person who offered any comfort at all. Back in September, Mr. Severs said, "After lunch, fifth period: a cruel time for English class. Put your heads down on your desks a few minutes while I read." Tiffany Barlow and Greta Hollingworth, the cheerleaders, giggled. "Sh," said Mr. Severs. "Just listen."

That first week, he read Greek myths. Standard fare for middle school: Athena springing from the head of her Olympian father; centaurs and satyrs, strange in-between beings, some of them wise, some of them not. The Minotaur, half-bull, half-man, wild, furious.

"Are they true, those stories?" she asked Jacob, a few days before he went away. They were playing Scrabble.

"In a way," he said. He put a Q on the triple letter box two horizontal squares before her feeble "it," and a U after that. She thought he'd quit there, but then he put an E down too. "The Greeks thought they were *quite* true."

She added up his score: forty-five. "But were they?"

"Well, what do you mean by 'true'? That's the question, isn't it?" he said. She put her X under his E and finished it with CEL on a double word square.

Jacob grinned. "Excellent, little genius. I'm still ahead, though."

"Not for long," she said.

"You think?" He put an A above her L, and two other letters down, and he waggled two fingers between himself and her: *ally*. "Twenty-two more points," he said. "Beat that! And while you're at it, answer me this: what do *you* think? Is there any way the Greek myths could be true?"

She waited. He always did this, posing a riddle with his older-brother grin, and then astounding her with an answer she couldn't possibly have thought of, but knew was – yes – right.

"Well, think about it. Is Christmas true? Are the stories in the Bible true? The gospels don't even tell the Christmas story the same way twice. How are we supposed to take that?"

"You can't ask a thing like that," she said. "You're going on a mission. You're supposed to *know*."

"Like Mr. Hartsough knows?" He winked. He knew how she hated Mr. H's facts, his Darwin's theory, humans descending from ameobas, fish, gorillas – look at the fossil proof! On the quiz, she'd written, "Dinosaurs, centaurs, minotaurs." Mr. H had the gall to write her answer up on the board, where, pointing in front of the whole class, he snorted, "That's *myth*. Those creatures – except for the dinosaurs – never existed. I'm talking about real species. *Real*." Tiffany Barlow inspected her turquoise fingernails. After class Caden

Corbin, the captain of the basketball team, wrote on the board, "Up*raur*ious!" Sammy hated them all.

But when Mr. Severs saw her scowl during lunch and got her to tell him about fourth period, he said, "Irritable reaching after reason," and "a fine isolated verisimilitude, caught from the Penetralium of mystery." Keats penned those words, he said, and Coleridge. Names from another century, another place. Mr. Severs said the first phrase was Mr. Hartsough's problem, the second, its solution. Sammy reported these luscious phrases to Jacob, who clenched a jubilant fist and then high-fived her. "See? Severs gets it. Keats and Coleridge get it. Truth's more than either dinosaurs or centaurs. The hymn says 'truth, the sum of existence, will weather the worst.' If Mr. Hartsough's the worst, we'll weather it just fine, I promise."

Now he was gone, and baby H sat stiffly beside her. Sammy scowled some more.

In October, Mr. Severs read Robert Frost. *Two roads diverged in a yellow wood, / And sorry I could not travel both / And be one traveler, long I stood / And looked down one as far as I could / To where it bent in the undergrowth . . .*

"Tell us what it means," the cheerleaders said.

"If you want to get at meaning," Mr. Severs said, "learn a word's provenance. 'Diverge' – 'di,' from Latin 'dis,' 'apart,' plus 'verger,' related to 'verse,' 'to bend or turn.'"

"Life diverges," Sammy wrote on Mr. Hartsough's next exam, unwilling to give it up. "Comes to a fork in the road. Men or beasts? Both, or either!" It could have worked like that. It didn't have to be one or the other, Darwin or myth. Both could be true in their own way. Couldn't they?

Black underlining scored Mr. Hartsough's response: "In this class, we talk *facts.*"

Facts, schmacts. Like Santa Claus is a fact? When she found out he wasn't, back when she was Mariel's age, she demanded of her parents, "So then is *God* real?" Their mother blinked, but their father said emphatically, "Yes, he is. Jesus is the most real thing there is, and don't you forget it."

"Remember that?" Jake said during that last Scrabble game, totaling the score, almost dead even, 105 to 104. "I can't *not* go on a mission with them saying that all our lives, now, can I?" A hundred and four weeks he would be gone. He would be twenty-one when he got back. So far away.

Three months ago, when he got the big envelope containing his official call to Colombia, their mother said, a cloud in her voice, "Aren't there drug cartels there? Guerrilla gangs? Danger?"

"He'll be all right." Their father put one arm around his wife, the other around his son. "They take very good care of the missionaries. They'll never put them in harm's way."

Sammy, looking into the future, saw two years of black hole. Outside the bay window, maples glowed red. Jake said, "I'll email every week." Once a week only could she write him her news back. It would be horrible. She laid her head on the counter, hiding her crumpling face.

"Be happy!" said their father. "We've been talking for years about when Jacob turns nineteen."

Then it had meant a hero in a dark suit with a name badge and companion. Weekly email descriptions of converts he would baptize as John baptized, with doves descending. But now that the time was here, Sammy saw the true meaning was *absence.*

She stared into the low mist surrounding the train, the green and red spotlights a dim glow off the track. When the beats between the wheels' clacks slowed and stopped, she stayed as close to Little H as she had to, as far as she could get, following the others a half dozen yards over the frozen pathway into the fire-warmed farm kitchen where, in summer and fall, the Callahan women canned peaches and stirred huge pots of boysenberry jelly.

Now one of the men, disguised in a curling beard and crimson robe fluttering in the sharp gusts from the open doorway, handed everyone a peppermint stick like an upside-down J and a homemade star cookie. Sammy waved these away, but Mariel took the sweets with a "thank you" and sucked at the candy ferociously.

"The stick is like a shepherd's crook," said Santa Claus. "This star shone over Jesus, newborn in the stable." Sammy wanted to say, *And – ?* But everyone else nodded. *Sure, right.* "Okay, everybody, reboard," Santa Callahan said jollily. "You're going now for a look at the *real* meaning of Christmas."

A look, Sammy knew, at paintings familiar to anyone who'd been to Sunday School, paintings laminated by the Callahans and set out on high easels protected from weather with light-festooned awnings, depicting the life of Jesus from Nativity to Crucifixion and beyond.

Mariel grabbed at Sammy's jacket as they made their way back to the caboose, stepping where Sammy stepped so as not to slip in the deepening snow. She sat close, invading Sammy's space. The startup rattled their neck bones, their chins in scarves, their mittened and pocketed hands. Lights aimed at each painting made hazy circles through the snow, falling thicker now, and colder. "O Holy Night" and then "The Hallelujah Chorus" wafted from hidden speakers.

The paintings loomed up, paused, passed by. Now the angel hovered in Mary's bedroom, the chosen girl's arm arched high against the light. Now pregnant Elizabeth reached to embrace Mary, while inside Elizabeth, John the Baptist leaped for joy. Through the snow, twelve-year-old Jesus stood among the elders in the temple, chestnut-haired in a robe and tasseled cap, threatening in his strange authority. Mary and Joseph hung back, observing. Mary clutched her heart. Sammy imagined her wondering: *Is there danger? Is he safe?*

In the first email from Colombia, Jacob said he and his companion had been mugged, their books and wallets stolen. "But we're all right. We're where we're supposed to be," he wrote. In another, he described dark figures, furtive and harsh, in a dim corner of the parking lot of the building where church members met. "We'll try to change their lives," he said. "We'll teach the world His truth." It was a code for Sammy, she knew it, another song they'd sung at church since childhood. In the third email, just two days ago, he said he had an appointment to meet with a spokesman for a guerrilla group. "Pablo's ready to make a change," Jacob wrote. "To choose the right." Their mother squinched her eyes shut, laying her cheek against their father's arm.

Now Sammy's eyes caught, unpredictably, a new picture, one she'd never seen. Spotlit, backgrounded by a folk carol whose words Sammy vaguely recalled (*wondering, wandering*), in this new picture, Jesus leaned against a doorway in the early dawn, eyes almost closed, calloused carpenter's hands at the collar of his robe. There was a worried look on his face, an anxious look. He seemed about as old as Jake, old enough for new hair on chin and cheeks, too thin to be a full-grown adult. Sammy felt she saw his thoughts pushing upward from his heart. *I'm the Christ? Really, Father? Me?*

Sammy sat forward to get a better look.

You're not kidding, are you. Whoa.

Rudely, she and Jacob had retitled most of the pictures in this Christmas ride, taking possession of them with homesick derision: Anna-nunciation. Stable-ity. John the Babba-tist. But this was new. She was curious. "Look," she said to Mariel. "What's that picture?"

Mariel turned, but she said, reasonably, given the worsening weather, "I can't see anything – what picture?"

Sure enough, when Sammy turned to point, she couldn't see it either. It was blotted out by marbling whorls of wind.

"Are we almost done?" Little H hunched into her parka, looking not for a painting but for warmth, kindness, rest.

Sammy sat back on the snow-cold bench, frustrated. That picture, the one she'd never seen before, was not about being "almost done." In the picture, Jesus was just beginning. He stood, like the man in the Robert Frost poem, where two roads diverged. Oh, there were no roads in the picture, just

56

that doorway, and Jesus, leaning. But Sammy knew what the two roads were. She'd heard the stories all those years in Sunday School. And here Jesus was, deciding: human, or more than that? Mortal, or god? Boy Jesus, or savior of mankind?

Sammy figured a title for the disappearing painting might be "Yellow Wood," though she had seen no yellow in the painting, and no wood, and no story in the Bible that she could remember corresponded to either that name or the painting itself. But everything about it made a certain sense.

Mariel mumbled something, shifted on the bench, buried her face in Sammy's lap. Practically asleep. No help there. *At the end we preferred to travel all night, / Sleeping in snatches, / With the voices singing in our ears, saying / That this was all folly.*

Folly, yes. There Jesus stood, gazing at his choices, looking for the meaning of his life. The facts. The lame and the blind, the dead waiting to be raised, the women at the well and in the crowd, trying to get something from him, water or virtue or whatever he had to give. Only misunderstandings ahead – people without ears to hear or eyes to see, timid leaders, oblivious men. He must have wondered, just in that moment of the picture, if there wasn't, please, another way, another road open to him, something less desolate than this crossroads. Were those his only choices? Unlistened-to God, or puny, earthbound man? Myth, or fact?

Sammy swiped at tears sliding out from her eyes for no good reason. It was too cold for this, too much to bear, these ridiculous impossible choices. She wiped her nose with the back of her hand and scraped the snot on her jeans. Mariel whimpered, her body a thin interruption of the wind in Sammy's freezing lap.

There were more paintings. Doves Distending. Water and Whine. (But Jesus never whined – these were just her and Jacob's silly words, not really funny at all.) Jairus's Daughter Undead. The Very Last Supper. Sammy saw them in varying degrees of dim and bright through the rising wind and snow, silly names for each serious scene, blurred colors and half-discernible shapes that might have been Jesus's donkey, bearing him to Jerusalem nearly at the end, or might have been his friends, bending low to try to find him in the empty tomb.

"Jesus was smart," she muttered, pushing the words toward the snowy floor of the caboose. "He went down *both* roads."

"What?" Mariel twisted her head, trying to hear through her hood.

"Jesus," Sammy said. Dead, but alive. Human, but God. Myth and fact. Both. No wonder he was so real.

Mariel squirmed. Sammy felt sorry for her. *Her* father said *facts* were the most real thing on earth. Poor thing.

Now cold stars showed between momentarily shattered clouds, the portraits wavering in the clear light and then fading into obscure blotches that could have been men on the road to Damascus or tongues of fire at Pentecost, while snow swallowed them again. The weather thickened, poured more abundantly, larger and larger flakes in super, superabundance. Abandon! Sammy could see less and less around her. It occurred to her that she never had seen much before, at all. She would have liked to say so to Jacob, or at least to Mr. Severs. But she could only keep still. Mariel slept heavily in her lap, as the disciples slept, waiting outside Gethsemane.

At last the train slowed, the time between wheel-ticks longer, and longer, and more long, until finally the engine stopped. Brought back from somewhere warm and light, Sammy blinked. It had seemed for a moment that Jacob stood in a yellow wood, waving and pointing to his name badge, mouthing the mystery he'd signed up for. She had no capacity to move.

In an uplift of snow at the end of the platform, two bear shapes appeared, Sammy's mother in her dark down coat and, near her, taller, Sammy's snow-covered father. Mr. Severs stood a little apart, clearly not a bear at all. *They've come to get me. How nice.* They stepped forward, gesturing. But she knew her parents, and there was bad news on their faces. Worry around their eyes. Mouths not smiling. Grievous tidings.

Hardly are those words out – she remembered lines from another poem – *when a shape with lion body and head of a man*, Mr. Severs had read it to them last week, something about slouching; and there it was, *something has happened to Jake*, slumping toward her in a hideous rush and then past, its teeth sharp, grimacing with the weather, an unbearable rough beast come round at last to put an end to everything.

O, this terrible, awful Christmas!

The railway car shook under her father's step and icy powder fell from his shoulders as, awkwardly, he bent to scoop Mariel from the bench. Sammy conjured a hooded creature, staggering and falling behind them on the rails, spilling Jacob's life down the tracks. Far away, in the background, children disembarked from the train. Teachers ushered them toward lit tables, where hot chocolate steamed and parents waited, and Mr. Severs murmured with another teacher. Through a buzzing in her head, she had the thought: *This may be the last moment left when anything is right.* In the rude shelter of the platform, her parents moved in slow motion.

I wanted to tell him about the yellow wood. She shook her head like some heavy polar creature, bringing onto her lap the snow accumulated on her shoulders and hood. *I never wanted him to go.*

Above her, on the platform, Mariel nestled against Sammy's father's chest. Mr. Severs came out of the whirling white, gesturing toward Sammy's father and the slouching burden he held. Her mother came to Sammy, lifting one booted foot after the other into the caboose, reaching for Sammy's hand as the stopped car swayed. Sammy could hardly open her mouth to ask the terrible question. But she must.

"Is Jake dead?"

Her mother stopped. "What?"

She couldn't say it again. "Jake – ?"

"No, no!" Her mother looked utterly startled. "Why would you think that?"

"Then what's wrong?"

The worry came back to her mother's face. "It's Mr. Hartsough. Mr. Hartsough had a heart attack and died. This afternoon in his office. He's dead."

Sammy gasped. She was sorry, so sorry for Mariel. *I had seen Birth and Death, but had thought they were different.* For herself, she could cry for relief.

"Mariel's mother's with the other children. Mr. Severs came to bring Mariel home. Your father and I were worried about the snow – "

"Let me see her," Sammy said, scrambling out of the caboose onto the platform. She maneuvered around her father, scoring the snow with her boots, shaking her hood and her bangs backward so that she could touch Mariel, little H who was still waking up, not yet aware, not yet knowing. What to tell her? What words to use? This would be harder than Santa Claus not being real, worse than Jacob being on a mission. Little H was looking down two hard roads, life and a dead father. She didn't yet know she'd have to go down both.

She patted Mariel's back, stroked her tousled hair, stringy with snow and hoody sweat. "You can do this," she wanted to say. "You have to." She wanted to tell Mariel – she wanted to tell *Jacob!* – everything she now knew. Mr. Severs held out one of his hands. Sammy pulled her jacket around her. Solemnly, their hands clasped tightly, adults and children stepped from the station into the bright, divided night.

Atar Hadari

The Empty Synagogue

In the empty synagogue
Praying the same prayers
Without the shuffling of the throng
Without the mutter of ten men

A small white bird
Appears on the ledge
And brushes with her small white wings
Crumbs from the edge.

The cloth on the tall box
And the names on the wall
Do not mean diddly squat
To the man saying nothing at all

Only the same names
Out of the blistering past
Only the small games
To make God rise out of the cards.

The man praying alone
In the empty synagogue
Talks on his own to his soul
Offers it up to God

As if on a petri dish
For some kind of random inspection—
But someone had better be home
When all those calls hit the system.

The man in the dark synagogue
Prays, the heavens are dark
And somewhere above or below
A spark, just a spark.

And somewhere above or below
Clouds turn in their sleep
And deep inside them a hand
Reaches out of the east

And somebody cries
And somebody says "amen"
And somebody tries
And the world opens like an oncoming train.

Aroma

The atheists go to their store
to mull over their devotions,
hunch over demi-tasse espressos
and leaf through all the papers

and clutch to favourite faded scarves
and watch light through the window
as wanderers go through the dark
to carry prayer shawls into dark halls

and electric lights go on
and standers-by and sitters
pray into the awful dark
for some way to distinguish

between the grimy light
and those moments of liquorice
those gossamer threads half sweet
that come and go in the distance

and sometimes catch before you go
in the turning ribbons—

The atheists go to their stores
to mull over their devotions
and wanderers walk through the dark
hoping for a way to keep their quotients

of light still in their slow
well meaning embraces,
the light from falling off their rugs
and sparks still in the work of tapestry
that glows in the cold fireplace.

Honey

You do not know what kind of day it is
till you try your fingers on a brick—
sometimes they crumble like buttermilk
cookies—sometimes you feel a little prick

against your fingers as you plunge your nails
into the entrails of the wall
you do not know at all how it will be
just that they'll fall:

and no sound but your heart beating for calm
anything for a little calm
sometimes you'll even chase their quiet women
the ones that look like calm is in their arms

but they just want to lie and wait
and lie and wait for love to turn from storm
to spring again and dew
never returns once it has burned in the noon.

So I stand here and run my hands
over the stubble on my lands
the only place I call my own
the skin between my brow and scalp

and when I've felt the hair
growing like land freshened with rain
I reach my hands again to the lion
in the wall and ask if he will again fill my hands

with gold so sweet it cannot be put down,
with that calm I felt when she once sprung my palms,
and then I'll feel these swim, like fishes, feel the lion grin
and all their walls turn into combs on fire with my pain.

Mr. Taylor

Even now I see Mr. Taylor
Walking over the water of wind strewn leaves
Streets on fire with left-over matter of summer
And not a spare man for all the trees—

Combing the streets for another face
To make up the quorum at Holy Law mornings
And not finding any trace of disgrace
In the fact that no-one willingly appears.

Walking and walking and never finding
And in his hands the names of members gone
And under his feet all their grandchildren
Leaves blowing away, the crumbs of a meal undone

And some of them red as apples,
Some just the colour of rust on wheels
And some just gone—it doesn't matter
Where they went—just that they will not come again.

And he walks over their rib-cage
The spine of the leaf that shows through light
And in his hands the names of their fathers
And in his heart a new name for the dark.

Prayers

In the days after my father's death
my mother prayed to him like an idol
to help her with her tears
to punish her run-away daughter-in-law,
and though she did not believe in God
she prayed to this unseen person
whose blanketed chest she had seen cold
with a candle beside, shovelled out of her bedroom

and still when she stays at night
she says there is no-one but his ghost
across the kitchen two place set
just his chair—no matter where she turns
and her room—that held the bed
and where he died—though lit with flowers
still seems too much over stuffed,
a space over-filled with memories—

and the corridor where she saw him last
in her dreams, is no longer white,
his towels, at last, she has reconciled
to take down from the bathroom's warming rack—

and the tub, where he's sometimes found
still in dreams, gleams
nearly unused now, exempt from his long showers
and she sits in his great armchair
waiting to see—if she stays up late,
if she's good, if she behaves herself
he will come home to her
and take the flowers from the bedroom wall
and make the coffee, and pull up a chair.

High Windows

If I had to define a religion
It would be the high windows
My mother put in the kitchen
Where there should have been a dining room ceiling;

ATAR HADARI

You could look up from your pork chop
Or glass of red wine and abandon
Just for a moment the small talk
And see yourself looking back down

Only with the night sky
undermining your belly
and light on the crystal glass
gold and older than afternoon films on the telly

as if you could see yourself
looking back with no sorrow
looking back at your upper half
and not feel a shadow

as if there was somebody up there
looking down at you
who knew what your thoughts were
and felt the stars as they wove—

but that ceiling was lost when we moved,
my mother took her flowers—
and now talks only of love
on the telephone and photograph enlargements

and I look over the heads
of my children and sometimes see women
moving, strong limbed and slow
across the plains in the ceiling.

And sometimes I see them glance
Into my face and the brilliance
Makes me close my eyes
And when I open them the child reappears.

And I see them do a dance
Reaching hands across the distance
Where my mother has gone long since
And I wait squinting into blinding rivers

And I see them turn and wave
Then dance again in a circle
And open again to the boys
Like an invitation to a miracle.

Healers

Ted Hughes wrote to you reluctantly
To give you the healer's number—
He said he had consulted him
I wonder now how often
And if he knew the wolf that closed
Its jaws across your larynx
Would bring its pearly whites to rest
Over his liver and thorax—
You never answered his last note
Nor saw the famous healer
Though I wonder now just what was lost
Behind your mouth, so tender
That it refused to mouth
Any but the basest profanities
Or the lip of the clarinet
That would play only the reediest melodies—
Nothing could be between
But life, toads and women
And in the large cool store

Your manuscripts laid for the nation
And underneath the scripts
In the hands of the shaman
A little brown duck that sailed the yard
And sported proud feathers,
So many more than you would ever countenance
Daring the world with its disappointments.

Silence

When I came to England, nearly eight
And walked to the neighbourhood school
Through the dark tunnel full of paint
And out to the leaves wet as wool

I came to the class of Mrs. Reynolds,
60 she must have been,
Hair dry as mistletoe hedge ice
And eyes squinted as if seeing the sun.

I sat while they said the Lord's Prayer
And did up my shoe-lace,
She came up and thumped me on the back,
"You'll not tie your shoe-laces while we pray."

And then walking away added,
"That prayer was written by King David.
You have no earthly reason not to say it."
I did not say anything

But sitting in the half-abandoned

PUZZLES OF FAITH AND PATTERNS OF DOUBT

Synagogue with assorted greybeards
And making up a makeshift ten
To read the law before the rebels run away

I sit, still, tying my lace
While they recite the Psalmist
And know in the heart of the light
There is what is required, what is artifice

And only the hours of light
Fleeting and through a cracked window
leave stains of gold on the cloth
the rest is memorial embroidery and wrinkles.

The Scar

Gary Guinn

In the moment of mute surprise after the pickup drove through the back wall of the church, and before the pandemonium that followed, Mary remembered the elephants in the Ringling Brothers' Circus and felt again the thrill of their sudden lumbering onto center stage. When Henry Swopes, the drummer in the worship band, was thrown into the third row of pews, Mary saw again the handsome young man in red, white, and blue, shot from the cannon over the line of elephants into the net.

Mary's husband Will, sitting on the front row, as he always did, leaned forward as if to pick up a penny, and collapsed onto the floor.

Through the dust and smoke and panicked voices, Mary made her way from her seat in the sixth pew, where she always sat, up to the third, to the side of Henry Swopes, lying face down as if he had fallen asleep there. When she knelt and took his hand, a moment of hesitation washed over her in the noise around her, with her husband Will on the floor beyond the first pew. The faint odor of mildew rose from Henry's shirt. Grease from the Exxon station lined his fingernails.

The sound of the ambulance in the distance rose above the voices of people in the sanctuary. Bobby Watson, a deacon in the church, stumbled up the three steps of the stage carrying a fire extinguisher into the smoke that seeped from under the crumpled hood of the pickup. Someone yelled, "Get that guy out of the truck." Bobby could not raise the hood, so he sprayed the extinguisher through the collapsed grill.

When the ambulance pulled into the church parking lot, the siren dying in a low growl, its red light flashed through the hole at the back of the stage and silhouetted the truck cab in the smoke. Someone helped Will up onto the front pew, his face and his shirt bloody. Mary slid away from Henry on the third pew. Will put his hand on the back of the pew to steady himself as an EMT, wearing rubber gloves, examined his forehead, gently pressing his thumb into the tissue around the cut.

Will's hands were clean, well manicured. He always wore gloves when he worked in the yard. Mary liked the feel of his soft hand absently rubbing her stomach as they lay in bed together. He was gentle, attentive to the things that gave her pleasure.

After returning from Kuwait in 1991, Henry Swopes had left his wife and two daughters in Oklahoma City and moved to the Ozarks to find peace. And he thought he had found it in the Midway Presbyterian Church. Henry's haunted eyes when he first testified at the church, the awful things he had seen and done in the war, had made the hair rise on the back of Mary's neck. When she went up to him after the service to offer comfort and gratitude, she took his warm hand in hers and looked into his moist eyes, then pulled his bowed head down onto her shoulder and hugged him like a penitent child.

There on the pew beside Mary, Henry began to snore. She wondered whether she could live with a man who snored. Will was a quiet sleeper.

When an EMT stepped into the third pew to look at Henry, Mary stood and moved up to the first pew and sat beside Will. She glanced back over her shoulder at the people. Some of the men herded their families toward the back doors. Some stood and stared at the pickup truck on the stage. Someone would have noticed her going to Henry on the third pew while Will lay injured on the floor. There would be talk. She took Will's free hand and pulled it into her lap. He turned and looked at her, his left eye covered with gauze wrapping, and smiled and squeezed her hand. She licked her handkerchief and dabbed at the blood still smeared on his chin.

The ambulance crew took Henry away in a neck brace, but Will refused to go. He said he would stay until everything was cleared up, and then Mary could bring him to the hospital to get checked. The stitches could wait an hour. He took his role as deacon seriously, as he did everything in his life.

A state trooper led the driver of the pickup, handcuffed, limping, out the side door into the parking lot. An ice chest half full of Milwaukee's Best sat on the stage floor beside the truck. Driving under the influence. It was an old story in Madison County.

When Henry Swopes had joined the church, his deep bass voice had been just what the choir needed. Not long after joining, Henry first took Mary home after choir practice when Will had to stay for the monthly deacon's meeting. Halfway home Mary said, though she didn't know him very well at the time, "Are you ever sorry you left your wife, Henry?" He looked at her across the open space of the front seat, and his hands tightened on the steering wheel. Without answering, he turned down the dirt lane that ran along the edge of Jack Barber's alfalfa hay field, pulled the car off the lane into a grove of pine trees, and turned off the engine. For one quiet moment, Mary was afraid. Her throat tightened, and she moved her hand to the door handle in the dark.

But in the silence, over the ticking of the engine as it cooled, Henry began to weep. "I'd never go back." His breaths came in quick pants. "Never." He pulled a handkerchief from his hip pocket and blew his nose, and the deep slushy sound seemed to suck all the oxygen out of the car. He looked over at her again, his eyes moist. She was sure, later, that the eyes were what did it. She pulled his head down onto her shoulder and, only mildly surprised, when he began to kiss her neck, she pressed her face into his hair. She smelled the mildew on his shirt even then. She and Henry made the same stop, there beside Jack Barber's alfalfa field, almost every other Wednesday night after that, Will busy with one meeting or another at the church.

As the state trooper led him away, the limping truck driver appeared confused, not sure what had happened. Like a fly in a spider web, caught in events he did not see coming, Mary thought. She tried to imagine herself behind the wheel in the truck, not sure how she got there, struggling to stay between the lines.

In the spring of 1990, Sophie Collins, driving under the influence, had run the stoplight at the corner of Douglas McArthur Avenue and Ridge Road just as Mary and Will's little boy Willie, riding his bicycle home from school, rolled through the intersection. Willie died before Mary and Will got to the hospital. The day Willie died seemed to Mary most of the time to be in the distant past, and yet in the half-waking of some early mornings it broke on her as if it were yesterday, and then she would try to remember what she had said to Willie that morning before school, after he knocked over his glass of milk at the breakfast table, as he had done so many times before. She might have said that she loved him even when he made her life harder than it ought to be. That even Jesus worried his parents sometimes. She might have said something like that, but she hadn't. She had told Willie he was driving her crazy, that accidents didn't just happen. That people were careless. As they came out of her mouth, she recognized with irritation some of Will's favorite phrases.

A reporter from the Gazette stood in front of Will, writing in his notebook. "We've asked the county a dozen times to put up a guard rail on that curve." Will reached up with his free hand and touched the bandage on his forehead. "It's a miracle nobody was killed."

He patted Mary's hand, which held his in her lap.

She would have to tell him everything. Maybe tonight when they got home from the hospital, before the gossip reached him. Her heart beat hard. She imagined him lying in bed, just drifting off. She would sit beside him and say his name quietly, with no emotion, the way people do when they are about to give you the bad news. The way the doctor had spoken when he sat down beside Will and Mary in the surgery waiting room at the County Hospital. When he had said their names, Mr. and Mrs. Biddings, they had known by the way he said it that Willie was gone. Mary was sick before the doctor could finish his sentence. A nurse rushed over to her with a basin, but it was too late.

Too late for Mary. Too late for Willie. As she ran her fingers over the knuckles of Will's hand while he talked to the reporter, Mary wondered if Will would know as soon as she said his name, the trick of her voice unavoidable in the gravity of the moment. Wondered if he would be sick before she could say what she had to say.

The state trooper's engine started up out in the parking lot, revved up two or three times, and the gravel crackled under the tires as he pulled onto the highway. The man in handcuffs sat in the back seat. Under the influence. Too late to escape the consequences.

Sophie Collins had been convicted of manslaughter for the death of Willie Biddings. When Mary thought of it, a ragged hole opened in her chest and dropped down into her stomach, tunneled down her legs into her toes. Sophie Collins had worked nights as a janitor at the school for twenty years. She still drove the 1966 Dodge panel truck her husband, a house painter, had used before he died. Mary had not talked to Sophie since the trial. Sophie no longer came out of her house during the day except for the Borderline Group at noon on Wednesdays. She had her groceries delivered.

A tow truck backed up to the rear of the church building, its rack of lights blinking through the gaping hole in the wall. All these flashing lights, now that the accident had happened.

Will stood up, steadied himself, took the steps to the stage slowly, and walked over to where Bobby Watson and Jimmy Counts, the pastor, a thin balding man with a protruding Adam's apple, stood by the cab of the truck. Bobby still held the fire extinguisher at his side. The three men looked down at the ice chest half full of beer as they spoke; then Will pointed to the hole in the wall, and Bobby nodded his head. Bobby glanced back over his shoulder at Mary. His eyes lingered before he turned back. Will shook both men's hands and patted Bobby on the shoulder. Will came down the steps from the stage carefully, his good eye cocked toward his feet.

"Let's go, Mare. Bobby's going to tack some plastic over that hole for tonight. We'll meet the deacons tomorrow and decide what to do about it."

Will had always been good in an emergency. When Willie was killed, Will took care of all the arrangements while Mary lay in the dark bedroom, half sleeping through the Valium. At the funeral the heavy smell of the flowers had made her sleepy, but he kept his arm around her shoulders, pulling her snug to him. At the cemetery he held her arm up against him.

Now as they walked down the center aisle of the sanctuary toward the double doors in back, leaving Bobby Watson standing by the ice chest watching the crumpled hood of the truck slide out of the hole in the wall into the darkness, she gripped Will's arm and tried to look past the bandage into his uncovered eye.

When they got to the car, Will laid his head back on the headrest and closed his eye. Mary drove to the hospital. With the windows down, the sound of the tires on the pavement and the smell of mown grass helped relax the muscles that had tightened in the back of Mary's neck. When they drove through a lazy snake of smoke drifting across the street from leaves burning in a ditch, she thought of Willie running around a smoldering pile waving a stick in the air, swatting at the smoke.

When they came to the dirt lane that ran along the edge of Jack Barber's alfalfa field, she slowed the car. Maybe this was the time and the place to tell Will everything. The scene of the crime. It would be quiet and dark in the pine grove. Maybe the smell of the pine needles and the bleak chirp of the crickets would help him understand why she had not resisted when Henry began to kiss her neck, when his hand began to fumble at the buttons of her dress. She might tell him that she could not breathe when she tried to remember the morning of the day Willie died. When she remembered the look in Willie's eyes just after he knocked over the glass and her failure tightened in her chest like a steel band. The simple act that would have cost so little, squandered, suffocating her.

When Henry had reached over to her in the sweet scent of pines and the sound of crickets, his eyes brimming, it had seemed at the time so small a price to pay, to breathe again for a little while.

When she braked to slow the car, Will lifted his head and groaned. He reached with both hands to hold the bandage at his forehead.

"You all right?"

He grunted and kept both hands at his head.

She couldn't stop now. He was in pain. And he needed the stitches. Her breathing slowed. She would have to tell him later.

At the hospital Mary parked in front of the sign that read Emergency Only. Will sat still, his eye closed and his hands in his lap, his head tilted forward.

"I'm dizzy." His speech was slow. "I'm going to need some help walking." He fumbled for the door handle, his hand shaking.

Mary had expected people in green scrubs to come running out to help, to see what the emergency was. But nobody came. The red letters over the emergency entrance seemed smaller than they had two years earlier, when she and Will had almost run into the glass doors that were so slow to open. She had raised her fist and pounded on the doors just before they slid apart. Blind machinery that wouldn't respond to her need to get to Willie lying somewhere in one of the cold rooms down the long hallway.

And beyond those doors, more machinery. Lights blinked on and off, tubes hung from plastic bags, the click and rasp of respirators forced cold air into passive lungs. Quiet voices drifted from behind the nurses' station. "Name?" A nurse had looked at the clipboard in front of her with eyes blank, revealing nothing. "He's in surgery. Second hallway on the left, waiting room on your right."

Will and Mary had barely sat down and gripped each other's hands when the doctor stepped through the door, drying his hands on a faded green towel. Not enough time to get ready. If they had only been able to talk, pace the hall, build up a fragile scaffolding of hope, to recognize the numb hand of despair as it slid into their belly and gave them strength. But the plastic seats were hardly warm when the words rushed to meet them. "Mr. and Mrs. Biddings."

Will stopped trying to open the car door and his hand dropped to his lap. "We'd better go in, Mare." He sat silent, his head bowed.

When Will had first started calling Mary "Mare" after the wedding, she had resented it. It seemed to reduce her, as if marriage had simplified her, stuffed her into a pigeonhole that did not require some part of who she had been before. But she had never complained and had grown used to it.

Beyond Will, through the car window and the emergency room doors, the hallway led past the emergency rooms to the surgery where Will had held Mary as she retched the day Willie died, where he had kept her from falling to the floor as the nurse patted her on the back and said over and over, "It's alright, Honey. It's alright."

Will had looked up at the doctor. "Is he?" The words had sunk dimly through the roaring in Mary's head as she retched, and she had known the doctor was nodding his head in the silence that lengthened and rolled over her. Then as quickly as it had come, the nausea left her, and she sat up and tried to remember what she had said to Willie that morning as she mopped up the milk that dripped through the crack between the halves of the table onto the floor.

"Can we see him?" she had said.

And Willie seemed to be sleeping as a nurse collected the

stainless steel implements from a table beside the bed. The sheet was pulled up to his shoulders, only a dark bruise on his temple and a scrape on his cheek. When Mary touched his shoulder, she felt the absence. He was not warm, and he was not yet cold. And the words ran through her head, *So then because you are lukewarm, neither cold nor hot, I will spew you out of my mouth.*

And Mary had laughed, a short huffing steam engine laugh that shook her as Will walked her back out to the waiting room. The doctor gave her Valium and offered a bed for the night at the hospital, but Will refused. He would need to make the arrangements.

Will leaned forward in the front seat and groaned. "Mare? I feel sick. Let's go."

Beyond the glass doors, a janitor pushed a dust mop down the hall.

"Do you need a wheelchair?" Mary said.

"No, I think I can do it if you're there to steady me."

They moved slowly. The doors slid open to let them pass. An orderly or male nurse, Mary wasn't sure which, saw them and came to meet them with a wheelchair. The young man rolled Will into the second room on the left and asked her to wait outside.

Mary moved the car to the parking lot. When she returned, a nurse in green scrubs, a stethoscope around her neck, brought the wheelchair back out into the hall.

She looked at Mary. "You look worn out. Sit in this if you like." She left the chair with her and went to the nurses' station.

Mary backed the wheelchair up to the wall and sat down. The hallway was quiet and not as cold as she remembered it. Two nurses stood at one end of the nurses' station talking. Another nurse leaned against the counter writing in a chart. Mary's eyes closed. The low whisper of the dust mop and the padding of tennis shoes passed in front of her.

At the trial Sophie Collins had wept quietly as the judge

pronounced the sentence. In the silence before the judge spoke, Mary had bitten her lower lip to keep from screaming. Willie was gone. Their only child. They wouldn't be having any more. Mary had seen to that. Once was enough to go through the wallowing heaviness and the pain. And now there was nothing to be done. She imagined Sophie wasting away in a dark prison cell, the shadow of the barred window slanting across her lap.

Then the judge's words had pressed onto her. Jail time suspended, driver's license suspended, Sophie's life simply suspended. Sophie looked up and caught Mary's eye, like a wounded animal in a trap, not struggling to get free.

Mary leaned her head back against the hospital wall and breathed the smell of disinfectant and human failure. She tried to picture Sophie Collins at that very moment in her darkened house, squat clapboard with peeling yellow paint on a bare lot. Mary felt short of breath. She had never imagined any future for herself except that she and Will would grow old together. Sleeping late on Saturdays, making love, coffee on the back porch. Weekday evenings, except for Wednesday night services, sitting together at home reading or watching T.V. Popcorn at the movies. Now she saw herself in some pale future, sitting alone in a darkened room lit only by the intermittent illumination from the television, eyes staring out of wrinkled flesh at the tube.

The air moved beside her, and she opened her eyes. A doctor stood at her elbow in a white lab coat, a clipboard in his hand. He looked down at Mary without expression and, his voice like tepid water, said, "Mrs. Biddings." Mary's stomach turned.

The nurse at the nurses' station stopped writing in the chart and looked over at Mary. The clock over the nurses' station said 9:37. The ten o'clock news would start in twenty-three minutes.

"We put fourteen stitches in your husband's forehead. It wasn't a very clean cut, so there might be a scar. Nothing he can't live with." The doctor paused for a moment. When Mary said nothing, he went on. "He's groggy, so we'll keep him here overnight. I don't think there's anything to worry about, but we want to be careful with a head injury."

He walked toward the nurses' station. "You can go in and see him now, but he may not be very alert. We'll move him to another room in a little while." He handed the clipboard to the nurse and spoke to her in a low voice.

The nurse watched the doctor's mouth as he talked, her eyes shy. She smiled and played with the pen in her hand.

Mary wondered whether Henry Swopes lay at that moment in a room down one of the other halls, chin held up straight by a neck brace. Snoring.

The curtain slid in its metal rail in the room behind Mary, and a nurse brought a stainless steel basin full of green towels and small scissors and tweezers and clamps out of the room.

Behind the curtain, Will slept. Instead of the gauze wrapped around his head, a square patch was taped above his right eye, a small dark spot at its center. The room smelled of alcohol and the brown disinfectant smeared on the skin around the edges of the bandage.

She would have to tell him about Henry tomorrow. He would sleep now through the night. She shouldn't disturb him. She reached out and squeezed his hand, soft and tan, but he did not respond. She wanted to touch the dressing on his forehead. She reached out and adjusted the sheet. He breathed quietly.

When she leaned down and kissed his cheek, the disinfectant smell rose to meet her. There would be a scar. Nothing he couldn't live with.

Leaning over him there, she imagined herself driving home past the Dairy Queen and the flea market, slowing when she came to Maple Street. She imagined herself turning left on Maple and slowing again at Sophie Collins' house. Sophie would be watching the ten o'clock news. She may have heard a report on the accident, maybe even seen video of the tow truck winching the pickup out of the hole in the wall.

Mary imagined herself turning into the gravel driveway, getting out of the car, and going to the door. She would knock softly, and at the sound of the knock, the volume on the T.V. would go down. After several seconds, Sophie's voice would come from the other side of the door, small and frightened by a night visitor. "Who is it?"

"It's me, Mary," Mary would say. She would reach out to touch the mute door face as a dry leaf skittered past her feet.

The silence beyond the door would lengthen, the ten o'clock news barely audible. The door handle would turn and click, and the door would open an inch or two, and one of Sophie's eyes would look at Mary.

"Mary," she would say, and she would look down and wait for Mary to speak.

Mary would stand in the shadow of the eve, the long shadow that stretched back two years to the morning she had spoken to Willie as she dropped the dish towel onto the pool of milk, Willie looking at the floor, saying nothing.

In the silence that would spread around Mary and Sophie, Mary would swallow and breathe deep and say, "May I come in?"

Sophie would step back, eyes still downcast, and let the door swing open in front of Mary. And Mary would step into the half-light of the living room and follow Sophie over to the couch.

Mary kissed Will's cheek again and whispered, "Sleep tight."

In the Details

W.C. Bamberger

I told the caller who interrupted my reading of the new issue of *Record Collector*, "I'm a veterinarian, not an ornithologist. The only *Ornithology* I know is Charlie Parker's bop classic." I didn't add that there are no ostriches in Vermont. At that point, I still assumed I was dealing with a reasonably intelligent man.

Father Nikolas Creel, the tinny voice on the phone, kept our conversation just this side of ridiculous the same way he later prevented me from feeling I'd been caught up in a community theatre *Da Vinci Code* – by being relentlessly good-natured. His end of the conversation didn't include actual pauses, only short interludes where he inserted dry laughter.

"Be that as it may, Dr. Mitchell, my friends and I believe you're the right man to help us with our ostrich question. We'll of course pay you – consultation fee plus mileage. I understand you have a new motorcycle."

"So spy satellites aren't a myth after all."

Father Nikki ("I'm semi-retired, so I use only half my name") said, "You're not being tracked, Dr. Mitchell, only befriended." He obviously enjoyed being a riddler; perhaps a habit carried over from the pulpit. He gave me directions to the small inn in Craftsbury Common where he lived, just under an hour from my practice in Adamant. You can't miss me if you come here. I'm the only vet on Sodom Pond Road.

"It's a nice ride," Father Nikki said, and one reason I finally decided to accept his vaguely *noir* invitation was that it was an excuse for a long ride. I nearly always have company in my van – gibbering, barking, howling company, and there's no escaping the smells, either. I'd bought my Valkyrie – 1520 cc's, flat six, as black and yellow as a wasp – so that now and

83

then I could get a little fresh air and remember the little details of how it feels to be human.

Father Nikki was right. It was a nice ride.

~

The mid-morning sun, as cool and white as bottled milk, lit up white clapboard of Craftsbury Common's famous octagonal band shell. The sails of two small boats on the blue glare of Elligo Scoloon were just visible beyond the inn. The same white Vermont light flooded the small dining room where Father Nikki and his friends sat waiting for me around a table with a shiny red and white checked tablecloth.

I am ashamed to admit it, but when I saw that Father Nikki was wheelchair bound I was irritated. It was as if his good humor over the phone had been a trick, that he had no right to be so cheerful. If it had been me, I knew, I would have been a fulltime S.O.B.

Father Nikki introduced me to the man seated to his right. Richard was a small, jug-eared man. He wore an untucked lumberjack shirt and a jute stingy-brim. His left arm rested protectively on two over-sized folders. They knew I already knew the third man. Benjamin is tall and barrel-chested, with pale, delicate hands. He summers in Calais, not far from Adamant. His six-toed white cat Lola is a summer charge of mine. Benjamin always compliments my Edith – a framed 10-inch LP of Edith Sitwell reading her poetry that hangs in my office. He would recite "The candle flame / Seemed a yellow pompion, / Sharp as a scorpion" in a startlingly accurate imitation of Sitwell's highbrow English bray. Benjamin had kindly signed a few original cast albums for me: he was a theatrical producer out of NYC.

The trio didn't waste any time getting to the business at hand.

"I – we – chose you to help us," Benjamin said, "for psychological reasons: Set a collec-*torr* to catch a collec-*torr*." Benjamin's baritone was as dark and deep as a cask, and he enjoyed manipulating it for dramatic effect.

Their story proceeded relay-fashion, each picking up the tale where he was at the center of the action. Father Nikki and Richard were well-known in the small world of Biblical manuscript collectors. They acted as agents for universities and museums, buying up papyri scraps and scrolls and cuneiform clay tablets, painted amphora, anything that preserved a text relating to Biblical history. Father Nikki's knowledge of texts was encyclopedic; Richard was a master of dialect subtleties – this was how they described themselves. "I'm the deep pockets," Benjamin said. Father Nikki had been approached, as he often was, by a man claiming to possess an important text; they had been skeptical, as they almost always were.

"He said his name was Mantikhoros," Benjamin said. He rolled his eyes. "I know a stage name when I hear one. He said it had come from a hidden room in a Syrian museum. It was all just *too* John Houston! But, I booked a first class seat and made First Contact."

"You flew into the Syrian war zone?"

"War zone?" Richard said with a laugh. "Benjamin? He never leaves the *time* zone. He flew to Manhattan. Brooklyn and Dearborn, Michigan are the new Cairos for collectors."

"I met Mantikhoros at an old furniture store in the Village," Benjamin said, scowling at Richard. "A plaque over the door read *Edgar Allen Poe Frequented a Dentist on These Premises*. Mantikhoros says he's Byzantine Greek. He has a thick black beard – talking to him is like talking into a black sheep's butt."

"Benjamin?" Father Nikki's tone was one of exasperation.

"Right. Mantikhoros told his story and let me look at the original – very beautiful; I *love* scraps – and gave me a scan to go."

Richard said, "The script is Koine – grunt labor's Greek in Biblical times. Jesus would have known it."

Benjamin interrupted: "Mantikhoros' daughter is a boutique rapper. She records personalized religious raps in Koine and streams them to aficionados at fifty bucks a hit."

"This kid wrote out a translation," Richard said. He slid the red folder toward me.

Inside was an 11-by-17 sheet of paper. On it was a pencil drawing of a shape like the outline of Alabama, filled with printed words. Under this was an 8-by-10 scan of a ragged yellow-gold papyrus on a blank white background. The drawing roughly duplicated the papyrus, twice-life-size. The block printing of the translation was gapped, following the tears of the original.

"It's passably fluent," Richard said. "An able girl. I am fluent, of course, but amended only one word: for *renanim* the Koine had 'hen,' but ostrich is correct." He shrugged. "She's young."

I read,

Yohannan . . . why the flea . . .
Only vex . . . lesson of cruelty, but Iesous
On the bank lifted . . .
The Ostrich rejoices in its wings, though its pinions lack vanes! Why?
She lays her eggs in sand. Why? Because God kept wisdom from

finding

Her, allowed her no understanding. Thus, Yohannan said,
Two questions are answered, but what of the third?
Iesous stared at the water, Third? The Dipper [hole]
Why does Yaweh keep the ostrich from wisdom? Those on the bank
Laughed. We are not told that she has no wisdom, But that he

deprived her

Of it, made her so foolish that she lays eggs where

they [hole] *crushed.*

Why? And why make her desert her young? Iesous

knelt. He

Wrote words in the sand, scuffed them.
Iesous said, Every living thing cannot have wisdom
To the same degree. If so, we would not be able to

teach one another.

Just as we look to God for wisdom, so other creatures

may look to us.

Ioesus stopped. He stared at the sand. No, rather I
say, we teach the
Ostrich nothing. She teaches us when we see her
foolishness. The same
Lessons from above and below, we [hole].
[W?] Ioesus fell silent, he kicked the sand. We
enslave her,
He said, steal her feathers and feed her meat to dogs.
This is because She
is foolish. We learn from her . . . Ioseus took a step
down. No.
Rather, foolishness is wisdom for . . . Yohannan . . .
Mocked . . . sand . . . D[?]

"A bad day at the shore," I said.

"The ostrich story is from Job, but I'm certain this scene is nowhere in scriptures or the known apocrypha," Father Nikki said. "Certain."

"Dr. Mitchell," Richard said, "do you know how an ostrich may 'rejoice' in its wings, even if she can't fly?"

I looked at Benjamin. He said, "You haven't picked up any bi*rrr*d psychology in your practice?"

Richard tried to pick up his thought. "It's because the verb can also mean . . ."

"What *matters* here is that this fragment shows uncertainty and confusion," Father Nikki cut in, his steady good nature gone. "Nowhere, *nowhere*" – he stabbed the checked tablecloth with his forefinger – "do we see an uncertain Jesus, not even in those moments when He is about to take on our burden."

Then Father Nikki suddenly smiled and began to wave, his hand flashing in and out of the striped light coming through the blinds on the south window.

Turning my head, I saw just outside the window an athletic-looking young woman with very long, tightly-curled corn-gold hair. Behind her three blond children were waving. The boy held a football, the older girl some electronic device, and the younger girl had ear buds like her mother's and stood very close to her hip. We all sketched quick waves and the group moved off toward the common.

"My great-niece Melissa and her children," Father Nikki said. "Visiting from New Hampshire." His smile faded. "Jesus taught through paradox," he said. "He was a master of riddles, the Word incarnate. This text makes Him look an uncertain fool, unable to answer a question. If it's genuine, this fallibility could shake some weaker folks' faith."

"Or make him more relatable," Benjamin said, in an uncharacteristically quiet voice.

Father Nikki's forefinger came down on the table again. "Jesus is not a cabaret character." He turned to me. "We need to determine whether this is genuine."

"You doubt it?"

"Fakes are everywhere – except perhaps," Father Nikki said, trying hard to imitate his previous good humor, "in the world of record collectors."

Richard tapped the scan. "Papyrus scraps like this are easy enough to come by, stolen from museums or from genizahs, chambers in synagogues where Jews have thrown used papers for centuries. They believe throwing away the Word of God is a sin, and some believe any writing a believer does naturally comes from God. Most scraps say something like, 'Tell Miriam to bring my sandals when she comes.' Some are even blank. But the ink, now, that's the telling detail."

Benjamin couldn't keep quiet any longer. "Red cinnabar ink," he said. "Mantikhoros showed me an analysis that said this ink is more than a thousand years old. We'll do our own, of course . . ."

"And if it's not a fake?" To me, this didn't seem monumental one way or the other.

Richard said, "If the word was the beginning, other words could end everything, don't you think?"

"You're the linguist here," Father Nikki said. "Benjamin is the dramatist. Kindly leave the drama to him."

"Loonies," Benjamin said. He held up a multicolored bag,

like a boy's marble bag. He reached inside, pulled out some coins and spread them out on the tablecloth. "Gas money." They were Canadian dollars, affectionately known as loonies because their backs are stamped with an image of the common loon. "Can*aaa*dian gas money," Benjamin rumbled.

"Why would I need Canadian gas money?"

"The man Mantikhoros is acting for lives between Magog and Shanks."

"In Quebec."

"That Magog; those very Shanks."

"Wait. Your source told you the seller's name?" In recording-collecting circles sources are jealousy protected.

Benjamin said, "His code of under-the-counter honor came in second to paternal pride. I've arranged for the rapper to come down to my studio and record a cabaret she's written – she calls it *A Dance with Sister Chance*. It seems Mantikhoros loves his daughter even more than money! Fatherhood is indeed a foreign country." Then he laughed so hard that he had a short but violent coughing fit.

"You're asking me to ride to Canada and find the source."

"Arthur Harriman, yes," Father Nikki said. "There's no melodrama here, Elio, no real danger. All we want you to do is to talk to Harriman and give us your impression. That's all. Anything that strikes you; you never know what details might be important to us. '*Le bon Dieu est dans le detail*,' as Flaubert said."

"Why would you think I would do this?"

"Loonies!" Benjamin announced loudly. He clearly loved the word. "There are a lot more where these came from. Or you can take it in Washingtons; two thousand of either. What's that in vet currency – eight cat neuterings with a couple of wormings on the side?"

"You three should go yourselves."

"I'm fluent in Hebrew, Aramaic, Ugaritic, Arabic . . ." Richard said. "I am surely on 'the list' with ICE." His expression and his tone made it clear that he was pleased by the idea.

"At the border I would of course have to follow tradition and declare *my genius*," Benjamin said. "Even I can't afford to pay that much duty." He held up a hand to keep the rest of us from speaking. He had noticed a serving cart appearing in the dining room doorway. "Thank you," he said, leaning back to allow the inn's owner to set out carafes and cups, then a glass dish with a glossy, untopped lemon pie. We were all quiet until she had closed the door behind herself.

"And my circumstance," Father Nikki said, patting the arms of his wheelchair, "makes it difficult for me to travel."

In a number of species, parent animals have learned to feign injury, to drag a wing or feign a limp to draw predators' attention from their young – a strategy easy to understand. What this bunch was protecting by doing the same I couldn't see.

"Harriman's front is a rare records business," Benjamin said. "You have an honest reason to visit him. It's not like we're asking you to *lie!*"

Richard smiled. "The two of you have had a lively email exchange over the past three weeks. He's expecting you this afternoon or in the morning. You've already told him you have a special interest in 1930s country blues and gospel singers." He took a few sheets of paper out of a second folder. "Copies of the emails. You mention Blind Mamie Forehand, Blind Lemon Jefferson, Blind Willie McTell . . . Benjamin has been copying down names from your conversations." They had obviously been planning this for some time.

"I'm not a detective," I said, but they could hear that I was weakening.

"And you're not an ornithologist!" Benjamin said. "With each offer we make you find out another thing you are *not*. Stick with us and eventually you'll find out what you indeed *are*."

"And," Father Nikki said, "I hear it's a nice ride."

~

I was sitting on my Valkyrie reading over "my" emails when the older of Father Nikki's great-nieces came toward me, one eye on the sidewalk, the other on the noisy game she was playing. "Hi. Can I ask you something?" Her long nose was decorated with a scattering of freckles.

"Sure."

"Is Great-Uncle Nikki okay now?"

Her mother and brother were on the Common throwing the football. Her younger sister was occupied with either free-style tumbling or first-year martial arts, it was hard to tell.

"He seemed fine to me."

"Okay, I don't mean is his health okay. I mean is he still crazy? This is a mental hospital, isn't it? My mother says no, but I don't believe her."

"He seemed okay that way, too. You think he's been crazy?"

Her mother called to her, "Stace! Come here, please."

The girl nodded, either at her mother, or me I wasn't sure which.

"I'm not supposed to know, but Great-Uncle Nikki sold his house back in Hanover to buy a piece of old paper he thinks everybody will want to read."

"Maybe he thinks it's a very important piece of paper."

"Okay, but Great-Uncle Nikki thinks people are still into *reading*. That's crazy isn't it?"

"Stace – *now!*" her mother called. The girl's jaw dropped, shaped the kind of thorough exasperation girls that age express so fluently.

"OK, thanks," she said. Her fingers had not stopped dancing on her game for one moment.

Maybe Father Nikki *was* crazy. I'd priced houses in Hanover.

~

I crossed at Beebe Plain, where the border slices the town in two - a neighbor's house might be in another country. I

91

rode north, Lake Memphremagog at times distantly visible to my left. English and French signs clashed in a crazed pidgin along the border, and then there's the bandana code established by the smuggler contingent. Uneven levels of taxation and regulation have spawned crazed flocks of transnational entrepreneurs on light dirt bikes that transport cheap cigarettes, Viagra and other staples of the good life from Canada to the U.S. They travel through the forests and leap over the highways. Red or blue bandanas tied to the uprights of a *Passage protege* or a *Bifurcation* mark their crossings.

No more than fifteen minutes out of Magog I saw a dangling mobile of sleeveless 45's hanging from a tall clothesline pole – Harriman's business sign. His place was a faded yellow A-Frame with tan shingles. Harriman appeared in the doorway as I parked my Valkyrie on the concrete slab next to a rusty, doorstop-shaped two-door and a mud-spattered dirt bike.

Record dealers tend to be an eccentric lot, and to occupy the extremes of physique – nerds with concave chests or tall fatties who shamble. Harriman was neither. He had muscle bulk that strained his black T. His head was shaved and shiny with baby oil, and he wore an inverted ship's anchor of facial hair: a handlebar moustache with a square plug of whiskers centered in the notch below his lower lip.

"Dr. Mitchell?" I nodded. "In here." He turned and went in. Not the chatty type, it seemed. I followed.

The far wall of the A-Frame was a triangle filled with vertical stripes – row over row of records, jackets and sleeves. In the small triangle at the very top rested the dough-roller shape of an Edison cylinder machine. I wondered if the original of the scanned papyrus might be secreted in one of those record jackets; a thief would never find it before dying of paper-cuts. One sidewall was banked end to end with bookcases, and any of those hundreds of books could be hollow, I thought; maybe all of them. And there must have been a triangular space behind those shelves.

"Country blues had a falling off," Harriman said, as he pointed to one of two chrome and vinyl chairs at a long pine-top table that held nothing but a brushed aluminum and black turntable. I sat down. "When the founders died, interest seemed to go down with them. But they're rising again. Where's your gaps?"

Performances of Indian ragas begin with the playing of the *alap*, a slow preliminary statement of the theme and variations, a kind of sketchy overture to the real performance. Our *alap* had begun.

"Good in Delta," I said.

"Everybody *thinks* they are. I've got a Charlie Patton alternate, with Bertha Lee."

"Nice, but I can't stand the way he sings, though I love to hear him talk. I don't care for lighter East Coast; Atlanta 12-string is okay; Barbecue Bob. But Tex-Arkana-Louisiana is what I'm after. Gappy there."

Harriman nodded. "I'll see what I can spare you." This concluded our *alap*.

Turning sideways in my chair to watch Harriman scanning his shelves, I noticed a blond maple lowboy directly behind me. In the low light I at first thought Harriman had a trophy football on the lowboy. I turned away. The only sports that interest me are the mutated kittens that sometimes appear in farm litters. Then a chill ran down my shoulders when I realized what I had actually seen.

"I've got to get to my workout," Harriman said, coming back to the table. "Let's start right at the top. I've only had this a month; you're the first customer to hear it." He slid a thick black 78 out of a clear sleeve and, holding it carefully by its edges, held it vertical for me to read. The label was plain white, with faded black hand-lettering. It read *Equip Check, Dallas, Dec. 5*. He put it on the turntable and set the needle in place.

There was an explosion of hissing, sharp snaps as the needle hit gouges in the shellac. The first sentence the blurred, gravely baritone voice uttered was chopped in half by a skip:

Georgia Rag isn't my number, that's a diff . . . ctell. That's his own number, and further that's a godless number. I sing gospel.

The speaker had a thick black accent, with a touch of a Western drawl much like Harriman's own. The voice was familiar, but I couldn't place it. Then there was a second man's voice, white-sounding and with an oddly pinched tone, saying something I couldn't make out. Both men laughed.

No, nothing against Georgia. I'm only saying it's no heaven on earth like Texas, especially up around Brenham, where I hail from.

As the needle moved across the 78 the hissing thinned. I could hear the deep rumble of the voice clearly now.

Hmm. I believe . . . I have only met one Georgia in all my life. Isn't that odd, now? Only the one. I was on the platform in Amarillo, 1917 or '18 . . . Now? There was the sound of a guitar being strummed. *Good? It was the day before Easter and I was trying to coax a little something from the passengers – to put in the poor box the next day, you understand.* The other man laughed. *I was singing "City of Refuge," like I'm going to do for you today, and I heard a woman's voice suddenly loud, blaspheming like a railroad guard. I said, "Sister, you shouldn't take the Lord's name in vain."* He laughed again. *I didn't hear right off that she was white, you . . .*

The voice suddenly sped up into a high blur, then stopped. A moment later it started up again at normal speed.

. . . the newspaper to the platform.

"It's right here," she said. I could hear her slapping at that paper. "New Drawings by Georgia O'Keats," at some place that had a number for a name, if my recall is correct. She was scalding hot – you know, the way only a woman can get?

In the background, faintly, I heard a woman laugh. The baritone had short, violent coughing fit, then his voice was clear again.

She went all on about it. "She was supposed to put them away, keep them safe, not show them to anybody," she was shouting. "Nobody asked me if they could show my work!" I told her, well, I had my own work to do . . . This was followed by the sound of a high sliding note from the guitar. *She went on blaspheming as she moved off. You can see how I w . . .*

The record revolved a few more times, then the needle began bouncing against the label. Harriman lifted it off. I sat thinking about that cough – and about what stood on the lowboy behind me.

"We've got a unique item here," Harriman said. "You know who that was?"

"Clues point to . . . Blind Willie Johnson."

Harriman nodded. "Guitar evangelist. 'City of Refuge' was his number, alright. Do you know who that Georgia was that he walking about?"

"Somebody named Keats."

"O'Keefe. He remembered that wrong. It was Georgia O'Keefe."

"The woman who painted flowers that look like sex."

"The very one. As always, the devil's in the details, and the internet says she was in Amarillo in 1918. This test proves Blind Willie Johnson met Georgia O'Keefe! Nobody knows that, nobody. I did a search before I bought this." He slid the record back into its clear sleeve. "This is a valuable test we have here, Elio. Smithsonian valuable."

"Just how valuable are you thinking?"

The price he named wouldn't have bought a house in Hanover, but it would have put a new engine in my Valkyrie.

Harriman glanced at his watch and stood up. "You can think it over in the garage. I've got to keep to my schedule." He started toward the front door and I followed. We walked down a gentle slope paved with pumpkin-colored paving stones that skirted a seep thick with broad-winged sedge.

"You deal in rare books?"

"No"

"That's quite a collection you have."

He looked back over his shoulder. "Did you ever read 'The Man without a Country'?"

"In elementary school. A soldier curses the U.S. so a judge

sentences him to spend his life at sea and to never again hear anything about the country. That story?"

"Right. When he dies they find he'd decorated his ship's cabin with everything American he could get his hands on."

We went into the garage through the side door. Light gleamed on chrome and stainless steel. Harriman's home gym filled the entire garage. There were racks of free weights, a rowing machine, a treadmill, machines with bars and cables stretching from one end to the other. Harriman lay down on the weight bench and began pressing the empty bar as a warm-up. Then he stood again and slid large black weights onto each end of the bar.

"Spot me," he said.

"You have those books because you're in exile?" I steadied the bar as he lifted it off the stand and pressed it a half dozen times.

"I'm fighting extradition," he said, between puffs of breath. "The workouts are just in case I lose and these Canucks send me back. A man's got to be prepared."

I felt another chill. "I didn't mean to get into your business."

"Oh, it's no secret," he said as he stood up again. "Anybody can read about it on the internet. Texas wants me, for aggravated assault." His expression and his tone made it clear that he was pleased by the idea. "I don't like being called a liar."

It came to me then that the Craftsbury Common gang had known all about this. "Sorry," I said.

Harriman added weights. "Don't be," he said, and lay back down on the bench. "Ask anything you want. I don't get much American conversation up here. Spot me."

I looked down at his sweating face, at the grimace that creased it with each lift. He was inviting me to ask questions, seemed at peace with being a fugitive. If it had been me, I knew, I would have acted very differently.

"Well, can I ask about that trophy on the lowboy? That's an

ostrich egg, isn't it?"

"An old one – more than fifteen hundred years old, in fact. You interested in antiquities? I'll give you a good price."

"There's a market for antique ostrich eggs?" *This* is why Benjamin chose me, I thought; I never know when to shut up.

"For antique anything. Especially from the Middle East. They emptied the eggs, painted them and used them as drinking cups." He rested the bar back in the stand. "The Egyptians thought of those big-ass birds as pottery excreting machines." He laughed, stood up and walked to a rowing machine. I followed.

"A drinking cup. I never would have thought of it."

"I bought it about a year ago, from the same dealer that sold me the Johnson test. He deals in a little of everything. When I was in Texas I used to fly up and meet him in Manhattan – in an empty building where Edgar Allen Poe used to go get his teeth drilled. But now he emails me scans. He thought he was selling me a candle. I could see in the scan that it was in good condition, with only slightly degraded clay feet. The decorative painting is poor – shaky lines, no focus; a sloppy job. But the top is a showstopper. Instead of the usual spout, the throat was sealed with a plug of red clay baked in the shape of a hat – flat-crowned, wide-brimmed, like a woman's sun hat. My dealer, or someone further up the line, had pried the stopper out and looked in, and thought the shell was filled with wax – someone had even tried to insert a modern wick. The dealer gave me a five percent tampering discount. An honest man." Harriman stopped rowing. "He knows he better be," he said.

He moved to the stationary bike.

"But it wasn't wax." He rubbed his fingers together. "It was silver-gray, and felt like the old-fashioned putty that used to come in rolls. I knew it wasn't a candle, so I ordered it. The day it came just happened to be Halloween, so I took the egg to the hospital in Magog."

"They x-rayed it for you."

"I told them the egg was left-over Easter candy and discrimination was against Canadian law." Harriman laughed. "The x-ray showed an amphora inside, a small jug with handles. A quick stop at a grocery for a nut pick, and I dug it out of that snotty goo. The amphora was baked clay, with a rosy tint. I picked the seal open and . . ." Harriman shook his head in wonder. "It was ink, and it was still liquid!"

"That's amazing," I said.

Harriman ran his hand over his shaved head, as if smoothing something back into place. "So amazing I wondered at first if it was a fake. So I paid to have it tested. It was genuine. So, yes, it is amazing. But," he stood up again and shook the tension out of his big shoulders, "no more amazing, in my opinion, than that Blind Willie test. And the Johnson's a bit cheaper. What do you say?"

"I don't know. There was that cough . . ." I'd heard that very same baritone cough, and recently.

"I know there's no music on it, but it's history, Elio, it's Americana; it's *important*. That's what you don't seem to understand here." An impatient edge was creeping into his voice.

"I'll have to think about it." Father Nikki might just have been wrong about the level of melodrama here, I thought. "You can ship it if I decide to take it?"

"You send the money and then we'll work out the details of when you can pick it up."

"You can't ship it to my address?"

"Making out a customs slip is not something I do. If you don't want to come back up here I've got a partner in Hanover. I can get it down to him and he'll hold it until you come get it."

"New Hampshire would work. I'll let you know." We started back up the pumpkin-colored walk. At the top I straddled my bike and searched for parting words. What I came up with was, "I hope you win your extradition fight."

"Thanks." Harriman grinned. "I think it'll come out my

way. I've made it clear to the Canucks that I have a few moves I can make if they get too cozy with the Texans."

"Moves?"

"Canadians all think Americans are barbarians. And there's this funny legal detail, Elio, that you might appreciate: Canada won't grant an extradition request if there's the possibility of a capital sentence."

"Texas wouldn't execute you for aggravated assault."

"No they wouldn't. But, if I commit murder in an American state that has capital punishment they'll never send me back. That's what the dirt bike is for," Harriman said, slapping its saddle. "Did you know that of all the states that border Quebec only New Hampshire still has the death penalty on its books?"

"You would do that?"

He shrugged. "What matters is that people have faith in me when I say I would. Let me know about that test."

I was glad the Valkyrie had electric start.

~

Once I was through Magog and Beebe Plain I parked in the sand on the side of the road and took out my cell phone.

"Benjamin? Elio here. Tell Father Nikki I said the scrap is genuine, that I have absolute faith in that. He's just going to have to be a man and take responsibility for introducing a little more doubt into the world. And two more things. First, you can keep your loonies; second, find your cat a new vet – Sodom Pond Road is closed to you. And, Benjamin? Go see somebody about that cough, and soon. I'm only a vet, but believe me when I tell you that cough could be the death of you."

Faith is like love: it does not let itself be forced.

Arthur Schopenhauer

Searching for Life on Mars

Andrea Vojtko

Nelson Mayfield was extremely fatigued. Just last week he turned thirty which meant he had already lived the average life span for a person with his lung condition. He searched for his next breath.

Lying in his recliner, he observed a squirrel outside his bedroom window sprinting up the trunk of a large oak tree. Its nimble body turned first one way, then pirouetted and fearlessly scampered upward to the topmost branches. Perhaps, my soul will end up in a squirrel, Nelson mused. How carefree to be a squirrel. They were so fleet of foot with so much energy, so agile and so bold.

"Nelson, sweetheart, how're you feeling this morning, dear?" His mother burst into his room with her usual cheer. He was disheartened when he saw she was wearing her large-brimmed red hat. It reminded him that she was traveling today. Her company in the Tech Corridor of Northern Virginia was always having these off-site weekend strategy sessions.

"I'm O.K. Just a little tired," he said. His once handsome face had thinned into shadowy hollows and his blond hair was trimmed in a buzz cut for easier maintenance.

"I've asked Serena and her mother to stay over the weekend so at least one of them is in the house at all times while I'm away."

"O.K., Mother. Don't worry about me."

"Are you sure you're alright?" his mother came over to the recliner and put her arms around him. She was a corporate executive working long hours, which often left Nelson in the inept hands of Serena, who spent most of her time in her basement live-in quarters visiting with her extended family – cousins, uncles, aunts. He had met more members of her family than his own. Nelson never mentioned this to his mother who had struggled with caring for him and going to work for so many years. His parents divorced when he was in high school – probably because of him, he suspected.

"Go. Go," he said kissing her. She gave him a long hug. He felt terrible this morning but didn't want to complicate her life any more than he had already.

When she left, he dragged himself out of the recliner and into his power-driven wheelchair. He motored over to his computer to get absorbed in something scientific, something emotionless. First, he opened his CD player and put in five CDs of Gregorian and medieval chants, which he found soothing as background music.

Nelson was an ace at computers and had achieved high honors in mathematics at Johns Hopkins when he was in better health, nearly completing his Ph.D. until his disease worsened and prevented his continuing at the university. Had he not been sick, he would have made a nice career in mathematics, but instead he used his skills to amuse himself on his computer.

He planned to use his own programmed software called "Zoom" to enlarge the live photos from Mars. Not only did his program enlarge sections of the surface of Mars, but it used advanced mathematical formulae to refine the enlarged pictures to eliminate graininess. He suspected he had built a better model than NASA to peruse the Martian photos.

He logged into his favorite scientific chat room on the Internet with his ID, "Airsupply." "Hi. I just logged on," he typed to his scientific Internet cronies. He coughed up some phlegm and threw the tissue in the large wastebasket next to his desk.

There were several people conversing on the Mars photos; nothing too interesting. He opened another computer window to start examining the photos. Using "Zoom" he zeroed in on one of the pictures and entertained himself for about twenty minutes looking around the surface of Mars. Out of the corner of his eye, he saw that the chat room had become very active so he scrolled through to see what was so important.

He read, "Get out of the chat room, Whizkid," "What a lot of bunk," and "This is for serious scientists." He scrolled back to see what Whizkid had said and found a line, "There's some kind of animal on Mars. What is it?" Then a response, "You must be drinking, Whizkid." A response from Whizkid read "I know what I see."

Nelson laughed at the scientists' furor over nothing. "What is the URL address, Whizkid?" he typed, while he tried to control a coughing spell. He was called Whizkid, too, when he was a young, budding scientist and he never liked being dismissed by condescending adults.

"What?" Whizkid responded.

"The address at the top of the window," he typed.

Eventually, an elaborate address came back and Nelson quickly entered it to bring up a window displaying a section of the Mars surface with a large crater surrounded by numerous rocks and crevices. NASA had installed a live camera on this section of Mars. He surveyed the entire area and didn't see anything amiss. He went back to the chat room and typed in "Whizkid, what does it look like to you?" In a few minutes a response came back, "Like a squirrel or a prairie dog darting around."

A squirrel? Preposterous, but he chuckled as he thought about the playful squirrel that morning. He wheezed trying to catch his breath.

A squirrel on Mars was of course ludicrous. Still he had nothing better to do, so he decided to pursue some modifications in his "Zoom" software that he had been contemplating for some time to check out what the Whizkid observed.

He heard a knock on his door. "Mr. Mayfield, I brought you your lunch," Serena said.

"Come in."

Serena entered the room avoiding eye contact with Nelson.

"Don't worry, Serena. I promise I won't die on your watch," Nelson joked.

"Oh, you are too young," she answered with feigned assurance.

Nelson suspected this was why Serena had so many of her relatives over while his mother traveled, and he didn't blame her.

"Just put it there," he said, "I'll eat it later." Serena paused as though she thought she should provide some greater service. She had very prominent cheek bones, large eyes and enormous lips, giving her the look of an ancient Incan, although she was only twenty eight. After she turned twenty five, her mother had given up on trying to find her a husband, thinking she was probably too exotic in appearance to attract a man in this country.

"Is it church music?" she smiled as she tied up the garbage bag in the wastebasket and put in another.

"Yes, I've become very religious, Serena." He looked over at his statue of Buddha in the corner. Serena followed his eyes and looked perplexed.

"I'm hedging my bets," he said; "I've decided to believe in all religions just in case one of them is right."

"Oh," she laughed and waved her hand at him as she hurried from the room.

He decided to have a little soup now that she had interrupted his programming, but he had difficulty swallowing it and went back to his computer. He continued working for another hour, coughing every few minutes and refilling the wastebasket with phlegm and blood-laced tissues.

After pausing a few minutes from his fatigue, he shook off his weariness and refocused on developing his code, adding several new formulae that would further refine his "Zoom" program. When he became consumed by the computer logic, he often lost all sense of time and bodily comforts. His breathing was becoming more and more labored as he neglected his medicine and lunch, but his mind was operating at an optimal level.

Finally he was ready to try the new program on the Mars photos "zooming in" on every inch of the frame. His eyes were fixed to his screen to see if there was anything at all in the live photo that was unusual. For one full hour he stared at the screen as his program surveyed the surface of Mars.

When the program completed, he came up with nothing, nothing at all. He knew this was a foolish pursuit but was still disheartened and wrote a message in the Chat Room to Whizkid. "No squirrels, Whizkid."

A message came back from Whizkid saying, "He's still there to the left of the big round crater."

Other messages crept in. "What's wrong with you, Airsupply?" "Why are you even looking?" "You're just encouraging him, Airsupply."

Nelson sighed. He was running out of options. He looked out the window and saw a squirrel jumping from branch to branch as though he were showing off for his audience. Who knows, he thought. Perhaps if he used differential geometry, the results might be different. He began feverishly working on this new idea, but after an hour he was interrupted by a knock on the door.

"Yes?" he said.

"It's Serena's Uncle Ernesto," a crusty voice answered. The door opened slightly and a short, muscular man with a handlebar moustache poked his head in. "I come for the tray."

"O.K. Come in," Nelson said. He had seen Uncle Ernesto on one other occasion when his mother hired him to do some plastering.

"Could I get something for you?" Uncle Ernesto said lingering.

"How about a new lung?" Nelson said with a smirk.

"Well, I know a man in Mexico who might be able to help you?" Uncle Ernesto arched his bushy eyebrows.

Nelson laughed, "Good one."

"This is music like in the cathedral," Uncle Ernesto gestured toward the CD player.

"I've become a monk," Nelson said.

Uncle Ernesto came over to him with the tray in one arm and placed his other large beefy hand on Nelson's shoulder bending down toward his wheelchair. "Play some mariachi music, man. This music is for Sunday morning."

"Well, I'm celebrating Sunday early," he said folding his two hands in prayer and bowing his head. Uncle Ernesto laughed and left with the tray.

Nelson continued with programming his new algorithm and in another hour tried it out on the surface of Mars.

Nothing.

He pounded his programming manual against his desk. "Sh--!"

he said. Nothing, not even an unusual rock or something. His mathematical nature drove him to find answers, but he thought it was time to give up. He was tiring himself out.

He wrote back to the Whizkid "There's nothing there, Whizkid. No squirrel."

"You mention that squirrel one more time, Airsupply, and you're officially banned from this Chat Room." "Don't be taking up our time with this nonsense." "Get a life."

He laughed, wishing he could get a life. A few tears rolled down his cheek and fell on his keyboard. He heard a tapping on the door and quickly dried his eyes. "Come in." It was Serena with her mother, Mama Rosario, bringing in his dinner. He had met Mama Rosario before. She reminded him of a soothsayer with her furtive head movements, hunched shoulders and black clothing from head to toe. Both she and Serena appeared a little shocked as they looked over at him. They tiptoed to the table and left his dinner.

"I do something for you?" Mama Rosario asked in her deep alto voice.

"No. Just leave it there," Nelson answered. But after his long day of programming, he had no energy to do anything and didn't touch the vegetable soup.

He went over to his Recliner and lay down for about an hour. Uncle Ernesto came back to pick up his tray and said, gesturing at the soup, "You didn't eat."

"Oh, just take it. I'm not hungry today," he said forcing himself to sit up.

Uncle Ernesto pulled over a hard backed chair and sat next to him. He took a chocolate bar out of his shirt pocket and slowly opened it up, breaking off a piece and giving it to Nelson. Nelson took the chocolate and put it into his mouth.

"This is the best chocolate in the world," Uncle Ernesto said with pride. There was Spanish wording on the wrapper.

"It's good," Nelson said.

Uncle Ernesto broke off another piece, "Good? It is like gold." He broke off another piece and gave it to Nelson. "Try another piece. It is made in Peru. My brother gets crates of food every day from Peru for his restaurant. So it is very fresh."

Nelson rolled the chocolate over his tongue to savor the smooth creaminess of the rich morsel. Slowly he ate the whole chocolate bar piece by piece as Uncle Ernesto fed it to him. Its velvety texture was comforting.

Uncle Ernesto patted him on the shoulder. "You have a good night, amigo," he said and left with the tray.

Nelson then dragged himself back to the computer. He still couldn't get the idea of the squirrel on Mars out of his mind. It somehow gave him hope that something else was out there.

He decided to run his program one more time, letting it step through each little piece of the photo inch by inch to see if anything would turn up. This might take some time but he would stare at that computer all night if he had to.

~

"Well, how's the Whizkid, this morning?" Harvey Fox popped his head into Edith Bleary's room at the Black Hills Assisted Living Center in Rapid City, South Dakota. It was mid-morning and she was on her computer, surfing the Web. Harvey was short, thin and wiry compared to Edith, who carried her 85 years with the girth and stability of a Plains pioneer woman.

"You won't believe what I found on Mars," she said to Harvey.

"Eh, you found something on Mars right here in South Dakota?" He went over by the computer that Edith's nephew installed for her. Though she was born in a South Dakota sod house, she wasn't afraid of modern technology. She had hitched up plows, worked the baler, the cultivator and been through more tornadoes than she could count. She wasn't about to let a teeny little computer scare her.

On her screen at least ten computer windows were opened, one of which was clearly a live photo of Mars.

"See, here, there's some kind of critter on Mars right there trying to get into the crater."

"Oh, yeh, I see. Isn't that something? And he gets in there, too. It looks more like a salamander or something like that to me."

"Yeh, or could be a prairie dog or a squirrel. Don't forget it's thousands of miles from Mars, so the picture will be fuzzy and all." Edith explained to him. "And the critters aren't going to be like on the prairie either. There's no grass there for one thing. Look how it crashes into that crater will you. I'm glad we don't have those things around here."

"Are you sure that picture is on Mars?" Harvey asked. He peered closer to the screen.

"Yes, see right there it says 'Mars.' Right there in the middle of this whole thing. Yeh, that's the address, they call it."

"Oh, yeh. I see now. Well, that's why you're the Whizkid." He looked close to the screen again. "Why does it print all of those other letters above the pictures?"

"Oh, that doesn't mean anything. There're a lot of funny names on these windows that don't mean anything sometimes. My nephew told me all this stuff is connected." She waved her hand back and forth across the screen.

"Oh, yeh. I don't know anything about computers. It's too much for an old Black Hills gold miner like me."

"They're not so hard when you get to know them," Edith said.

Harvey leaned closer to the computer screen. "Is that Mars?" he asked again.

"It does look peculiar, don't it?"

He shrugged his shoulders and grinned. "I don't want to tell you what it looks like to me," he said with a wink.

"I don't want to hear, you old coot. I know the way you think. It's Sunday, you know. I want to see you at the church service this afternoon."

"O.K. I'll be there praying for my sins." Harvey chuckled and left her to her Web surfing.

~

"Whizkid, send me your E-Mail address. I'll give you mine. I have some questions." Nelson typed his E-Mail into the Chat Room. He had not slept all night, staring at the screen as though it were an oracle. After about ten minutes he got an E-Mail from EBleary. He sent her another E-Mail with specific instructions to get the address of the window she was looking at. After several E-

Mails back and forth he got an address different from the original Mars window.

Nelson typed it in and began coughing vigorously as he saw a demo of a sperm piercing into the wall of an egg on a family planning site. The crater in the Mars photo did bear a resemblance to the circular egg in the demo, even the burnt sienna coloring was the same in both windows. He put his sunken cheeks into his two bony hands and began sobbing. It was nine o'clock on Sunday morning and he heard a knock on his door. He said, "Come in," but when Serena entered with his food he continued to sob, blowing his nose and coughing intermittently. Serena said, "Are you O.K., Mr. Mayfield?" He continued to cough and cry. Serena tried to hand him a tissue but he ignored her and she finally ran out of the room. He had no energy left. What was he thinking, looking for a squirrel on Mars? He laughed sardonically. He was not squirrel material in this life or an afterlife.

Several minutes later he could hear Serena, Mama Rosario, and Uncle Ernesto outside the door talking in hushed tones with each other. He tried to control his coughing, blow his nose and wipe his eyes and then said, "Come in." A few minutes passed while the whispering outside his door continued. Finally Uncle Ernesto entered carrying a banged-up portable tape deck. He went over to the CD player and pressed the power button off.

"Here's something to make you feel better," Uncle Ernesto said. He pressed a few buttons on the tape deck and a Mariachi band played a lively Mexican song in Spanish.

Nelson turned and looked at Uncle Ernesto who was smiling broadly at him while swaying back and forth to the music. He came over and put his muscular arm around Nelson's thin shoulders. "This is better to listen to. Believe me."

Nelson felt a warm feeling go through his body from Uncle Ernesto's hug. He began to move gently to the Mariachi music along with Uncle Ernesto. Nelson turned to Uncle Ernesto and said softly, "Thank you." And then looking into his eyes added, "I do believe you."

Modest doubt is call'd the beacon of the wise.

William Shakespeare

Bill Scalia

Dawn, Day 1

Three broad leaves
Fall at my door
Faith, Hope, Love—
But the greatest of these—
Is trees

When God Called Adam from the Dirt

When God called Adam from the dirt
He made ribs from catfish bones
He made the heart from *sac-au-lait*
He made brains from mossy mud and
He made Eve from just the same
He drew her from the fertile soil
He gave her life with steaming air
Like dew from magnolia blossoms

When Adam heard the sound of the Lord walking in the
world

He knew the silence of his mind.
He saw Eve new in his affection.
He saw the land live in the measure of his sight.
He saw children, and he saw a mother,
And he heard their melodic voices on the hot wind.

When God expelled Adam and Eve,

They went downriver.
They rafted to the lower Mississippi.
They settled in the river delta.
They found their work-land, and they were home.

Adam farmed and fished and sweated.
Eve worked the garden and tended the animals.
Able was murdered in the fields.
Cain left home, running from the law.

Their descendants live on in deep Louisiana.
You know them by their muddy hue and their poverty,
By their brown eyes and mossy hair,
And by their desperate laughter, like music on the hot wind.

The Mass of Pallas Athena

I had been watching a bird fluttering in the northwest corner
of the church, small and brown, a parking lot bird, when I
noticed her. The woman stood in the row in front of me,
three people to my right, so that I had an oblique view of her.
She was tall and of a stately mien. That is, she seemed
perfectly put-together. That expression is my mother's. *Put-
together*. I always took it to mean that a woman is of exactitude
appropriate to her condition, status, class, purpose. This
woman was *put-together*, seemingly by an internal, inscrutable
purpose of self. She knew herself, it seemed to me.

Her hair was long, and sandy-blonde, and fell in a perfect slow
wave over her wheat blouse like goats moving on the slopes
of Gilead. In profile she seemed less evolved than sculpted,

less organic than created, in contract with a Titan craftsman. Her grey-blue eyes might have been Athena's. Her skin was clear and cool.

I noticed her because it was impossible for me not to, in the way that people notice in others the vacancies in themselves. Maybe no one else saw her at all. I looked until I couldn't look anymore, out of embarrassment.

I didn't receive communion, so I stood aside at the end of the row to let others pass, their heads bowed. As she walked by, my head lowered so as not to confront the solemnity of the occasion, I noticed a Band-Aid on her left hand, around the end of the ring finger. The Olympic perfection I had sensed in her was jarred by the single evidence that she was not, after all, inscrutable, and so sang my heart. She was elevated in my sight. I knew something authentic, perhaps for the first time, in that communion of strangers.

Intercession (The Authenticity Dream)

I walk a dirt road, and as I walk people begin to fall in behind me. Why, I don't know. The road becomes hilly, small and steep hills, so I have the sensation of rising and falling. More people fall in, and a crowd develops. The hills get bigger. Then, on the tops of the hills, I see telescopes, one on top of each hill, on each side of the road. The telescopes are all pointed in the same direction of the sky, at the same angle. Many miles of road. Hundreds of telescopes.

I come to one very large hill. I climb it, along with the crowd behind me. It's a long climb, but as I reach the top, the hill flattens into a field of long grasses, swaying gently, the breeze moving over the ground like waves. Now it's beautiful, the sun is shining, and I feel good and happy, like I have a purpose, though I don't know what it is.

Inspired, I start directing people to tasks. "Bring lumber," I order one group, and though I don't specify dimensions, they seem to know. "We'll put the large post here," I call, pointing to a specific spot. "Then we'll nail the cross beam." I watch a group of people dig a hole for the post, and visualize the structure. I'm building a cross. I'm heading up a crucifixion.

Just then, at the height of my labor, I notice a small cloud, up and to my right. The cloud *wasn't* there, and then just *was*; it simply appeared from nowhere, and originated exactly in the place the telescopes were pointing. The cloud moves, slowly at first, then gains speed and dimension, becoming tubular. It moves across the sky, right to left, cuts toward the ground, but before it reaches the ground it takes another turn, and heads for me.

"Is that cloud for you?" someone asks, and I laugh. I turn to answer, but I have no answer. When I turn back, the cloud is on me, and then around me. I am inside the cloud. Nothing else is there, not the crowd, the field, the cross, nothing, just *me* and *not-me*. I'm boiling hot and my eyes won't close. A face appears *in* the cloud, *of* the cloud, a face I can't describe, with the attributes of something I recognize as a face, but without specific features. It has the face*ness* of a face, without the face.

And then it speaks. I can't hear it. The voice has the sound*ness* of a voice, but without the sound, and it says: *In half your life, you have not done enough for me.* I can't move, or close my eyes, or

114

tune out the voice. Then my vision is obscured. I haven't
closed my eyes, but I've been blinded, and I can only see
words written in the air, in the cloud. The words are the same:
In half your life, you have not done enough for me.

The Revival

As a child I saw a tent revival preacher
Hammer at his bible
Shouting lamentations and punishments
For all us miserable sinners,
Whose foot shall slide in due time

As he defiantly strode the stage,
He smote the open book with his palm, and
Leaves tore from the spine, fluttering to the ground,
Like the wings of failing doves

These dying wings
Emblems of our failure
Were sadder to me than the implications of torture

When I got home I looked in my father's bible
And saw the pages intact,
Their wings folded again,
Ready to bear the weight of me

I thought about this thing,
And something came to me, as to one born abnormally,
And I *knew* it,
As bread knows the earth, or
As blood knows the heart.

Vastation

Soft in the void of a velvet sleep
I saw a great, white light open before me.
The light pulled me forward in three slow waves.
I saw the light, felt the comfort of the light, and then I was
                                                    inside the light;
my mind contracted and convulsed, pulsed in the depths
between compaction and expansion,
      and I awoke, *knowing*.
In the design of the universe, meaning lives in the house of
                                                    mystery.
Three times I tried to wrap the vastation in words, and
three times it slipped away, like a shade, to the underworld.

The End of Time

Time stretches behind me as I drive in the mephitic August
                                                    night.
Wretched heat warps the air.
Asphalt steams, out-gassing, silver-blue in the colossal head of
                                                    the full moon.
I smell the great river from the highway, up past Jackson, a
                                          pungent muddy, brown fish
smell, like creation.

In north Mississippi, south of Memphis, I-55 becomes
                                    violence, painted red-black
with blood.
Ribs shine white, arched like a whale's, standing above a bull's
                                                    carcass.

The animal spreads an entire lane, midstripe to shoulder.

The clock reads 11:11 - - *1111* - - the tumblers slide into place:

I see a man in need, prone on the shoulder of the
                                    highway, stretched beside his
car, and I steer to the side of the road.
I run down the hot highway's shoulder.
He rises to meet me.
I see him in the lights of an oncoming car.
Then I see fate, like a thick black wave.
The sound crushes me, and
then all stopped.
The man in the road looks at me still, his bluish-gray eyes
                                            wide open.
His spine is snapped through his shirt.
His head is cracked open like an egg.
His brain lay at my bare feet.

God stopped time, right there in Mississippi, on that night.
God's off hand reached down and pulled back the curtain and
                                            showed me
    the world behind the mask.
Death, the fashioning animus, the skulking machine, clean and
                                white, odorless, timeless,
    destroyer of the senses.

This is the way things are, the difference between be and seem.

Then the curtain closed and the stage restructured itself.
Sounds crawled back, slowly, the wind, cars, crickets, frogs.
Palsied, time cranked forward.

Daybreak, on the road, and on the pink-red skin of the sky

The sun puffs up like a blister.
I can't tell the time because God changed the dialplate.
Heat burns through the cracks, between time and the world,
red blazing through a wobbly
　　　furnace.
If the proofs were proved and God presented himself, nothing would be
　　　　　　　　　　　　　　　　　　　　changed, and I
　　　became hotly aware that all was exact in the mere fact of
　　　　　　　　　　　　　　　　　　　　the world.

The morning heat blurs yellow waves into fired slurry, making
　　　　　　　　　　　　　　　　focus impossible, and I drive,
　　　unknowing, home, hoping that home is still home.

Pumpkin Patch

Edie Cottrell

Jonathan stole a glance at his father who was pacing back and forth on the well-worn carpet. The boy was rummaging in the entry closet of his dad's tiny bachelor apartment. Two weeks ago, he'd dumped his cleats and baseball glove and raced out the front door. His mom had already driven up, and he couldn't wait to get back to her house on the other side of town.

"If we're not out of here in two minutes, we won't have time to stop at McDonald's," Fred Adams yelled. "How can you expect to play a good game if you don't eat breakfast?"

Jonathan spied the misplaced shoe and retrieved it as his father towered over him. Just for once, he wished he could spend the weekend with his dad and not have to hear that angry voice. Just for once, he wished things could be different.

They drove along the early morning streets in silence. The beat-up Ford Escort whisked them along Old Highway Road past the boarded-up storefronts of J.C. Penny's and Al's Barber shop. Al had died, Jonathan knew that, but he wondered what had happened to Penny's. Last week, his fourth-grade class had collected canned goods for the homeless people camped out near the pier outside of Red Wolf. He wanted to tell his father it seemed kind of sad for these old, abandoned buildings to sit empty when folks needed a roof over their heads. But his parents were always saying he shouldn't worry about things that didn't concern him.

At McDonald's, Jonathan wolfed down his food. At least, he could always count on his dad to take him out to eat. His mom would never even step foot in a fast-food restaurant. If he had his way, he'd gulp down the greasy sausages and biscuits slathered with honey every day, but the scrambled eggs were another story. He had to force himself to swallow the lukewarm, washed-out yellow clumps.

"All through," he announced.

Fred pushed aside the napkin Jonathan had used to cover the plate. "I've told you not to leave your eggs."

"Aw, Dad, I ate most of them." He poked the plastic fork into the last scattered bits.

"What is it with you, Jonathan? Are you stupid or what?"

The boy shrugged.

"Answer me when I speak to you."

"Yes, sir."

"I mean what I'm saying now. For Pete's sake, you're almost ten years old! I shouldn't have to force you to eat. We're going to be late for *your* game, but we don't leave till you clean your plate."

When Jonathan saw several other customers turn and look their way, he shoved the last bites into his mouth. Why did his dad have to be like this? He looked down at his plate and blinked hard to hide his tears. He couldn't stand to be called a crybaby, especially by his father.

No matter how much he tried, it seemed he could never please the man. It didn't matter one bit, either, what his mom said. *Things change, Jonathan. You'll see when you get older. Your dad's hard on you because he wants you to be good. And don't forget: God is watching over you.*

Ha! Like she could talk! She wouldn't even *live* in the same house with her own husband. Now, when anyone asked, he had to admit his mom and dad were divorced. Where was God when they'd made *that* decision; that's what he'd like to know.

As they drove beyond the outskirts of Red Wolf, the traffic thinned out, and Old Highway Road quickly turned into two narrow lanes. Jonathan peered out the window at the rich Texas Hill Country. Even near the end of October, the colorful patchwork mosaic was still dotted with lush green squares and the occasional lavender one.

At that moment, he spied a bright orange rectangle in the design.

"Dad, look!"

"What? Why must you yell like that in the car?"

Jonathan pointed to the field.

"So?"

"It's a pumpkin patch! It's gotta be. Can we stop on the way back from the game? Please, Dad, can we, please?"

"Aren't you a bit old for jack-o-lanterns and Halloween?"

Jonathan considered the possibility. "I don't think so," he said. "Please, can we stop?"

"Jack-o-lanterns are for sissies. Besides, you should be concentrating all your energy on the game now. You hear me? No more nonsense about pumpkins."

Jonathan turned his back on his father and stared out the window at a barren stretch of earth. Why couldn't his dad be like everyone else's? What would be so wrong if they stopped and bought a stupid old pumpkin?

When they pulled into the parking lot beside the baseball diamond, Jonathan could see his teammates already assembled on the field. He grabbed his cleats and glove and raced from the car without saying goodbye.

~

By the bottom of the seventh inning, Jonathan had singled twice, doubled on a hit that drove in a run, and fielded all but one ball that had come his way. As he waited for the pitch, there were two outs and a player on third. The count was two and two. If ever the moment had come when he needed to remember everything his father had taught him, this was it.

The pitcher threw a fast ball that whizzed by, just barely inside.

Jonathan swung hard, too hard, and missed.

"What the hell was that?" Fred shouted from the bleachers.

Even from home plate, Jonathan could see the angry red face, the clenched fists.

"Why'd you swing so soon? Haven't I taught you to watch the ball?"

The boy looked over at his coach. He knew that league rules prohibited parents from sideline coaching. The coach motioned for Jonathan to take his fielding position at second base.

"I'm talking to you, son. Don't you walk away!"

Jonathan watched one of the other fathers hurry over to his dad.

"Who the hell do you think you are?" Fred turned on the man and jerked his arm free. He charged to the edge of the playing field. "If I were your coach, I'd take you out of the game for good. You don't deserve to play."

It was all Jonathan could do to keep from crying. It was bad enough when his father tore him down at home. But here he was with every one of his teammates, every parent in the crowd, staring right at him. His legs felt like rubber; his head throbbed. What was the point trying his best to make his father proud of him? He was a good kid, he really was. Yet his dad hated him, so he hated his dad right back.

Jonathan ran as fast as his legs would carry him to the parking lot. Right this second, even the ugly Ford Escort looked pretty good. He jerked first one door handle and then another.

"Stupid old car!"

He slumped to the ground and buried his head in his arms. It didn't matter what his mom said. God didn't care what happened to him. Not one bit! He might as well be one of those homeless people out by the pier.

When he heard footsteps, he didn't even look up.

"Get out of here!" he cried. "I hate you! I hate you! I hate you!"

"Don't you dare speak to me like that!"

"How could you yell at me in front of all the guys? I'll never talk to you again – not ever! You'll see. And I'll never play baseball – not ever so long as I live!"

Fred grabbed his son by the shoulders. "Stop this nonsense and get yourself back out there on that field!"

Jonathan broke free and headed for the open road. He wanted to leave the field far behind. His father had gone too far this time. He'd *never* forgive him. Never! Not in a million years.

The screech of tires pierced the still air as the car tore out of the parking lot onto the dirt road. A cloud of dust surrounded the boy.

"Get into this car, Jonathan!"

He shook his head *No*, speeding up his pace.

"All right then, go ahead and run off your temper tantrum. See if I care!"

He'd never defied his father like this. He hesitated only long enough to glare into the car before heading for the other side of the road. There! Take that. Bet you're too chicken to cross over the line.

It was only when his legs could no longer sustain the momentum that Jonathan finally dropped to the ground. He heard the Escort brake behind him. But when his dad tried to help him up, Jonathan threw off the big hands and hobbled to the car on his own. He hurled himself into the backseat.

"Jonathan, listen to me. You need to stop feeling sorry for yourself and get back to your team."

"What're you gonna do – force me?"

"Enough of your sass! Not another word." Fred peeled off onto the open road.

Jonathan risked a peek into the rearview mirror where he studied his father's image. What he saw was a weathered version of his own face. Twenty-five years from now, that's what he'd look like – all except for the piercing blue eyes he'd inherited from his mother.

They were about halfway home when Jonathan glanced in the mirror again and realized his father was trying to make eye contact. What did he care?

Just then, he noticed the patch of bright orange in the not

too distant landscape.

"Do you still want to stop and buy a pumpkin?"

In the last half hour, Jonathan had worked hard to convince himself that nothing mattered. Hadn't his dad insisted he was too old for Jack-o-lanterns? Why should he pretend to care about such a stupid thing as Halloween? He was through with being a kid. Things change, all right, *Mom.* Humph! He didn't need a father any more than she needed a husband.

"Jonathan, talk to me, damn it! Do you want to stop?"

The car lurched into the parking area in front of the pumpkin patch and screeched to a halt.

"Out!" Fred yanked open the backseat door.

Jonathan stood there while his father began to make his way among the irregular rows of pumpkins. He'd show his dad a thing or two, all right. He wouldn't even *look* at the stupid old pumpkins.

"Here, son, how about this one? Or this lopsided one? It's got personality. What do you say?"

It's got personality. Like I care.

Fred pointed to a group of younger children all dressed up in Halloween costumes.

"Tell me, what're you going to be for Halloween?"

Jonathan stared straight ahead. He couldn't believe what was happening. If he didn't know better, he'd swear his dad was actually trying to make up. Well, too bad! He wouldn't give in. Not after the way his father had embarrassed him.

"Come on now, son."

Jonathan stayed right where he was. He was trying to figure something out. When his father turned in the same direction, the boy motioned for him to stop.

"Wait," he said as his dad approached. "Don't stare."

"What is it?"

"I don't know. I wondered if maybe it was a costume, but I don't *think* so. Look, Dad, he's turned away. Let's walk over there."

Jonathan headed to the right into a maze of haystacks with

his father trailing him. They both stopped all at once. Up ahead stood a strange figure dressed in baggy jeans and a ragged plaid shirt with the sleeves hacked off. From the back, all they could make out was his long, unkempt, graying hair and his peculiar, erratic movements. As they walked on, he suddenly turned to stare right back at them. It was the father who almost called out, but Jonathan grabbed his hand.

"Is it a costume?" Jonathan whispered after the man had lumbered past them.

"I don't think so."

"What's *wrong* with him?" Jonathan held tight to his father's hand.

"I don't know, I don't know. Sometimes things in nature go terribly wrong. I guess that's just the way he is."

"What's that *thing* on his back? Is that what they call a hunchback?"

"Yes, at least, I think so."

"How can he be so short? He's not even as tall as I am, but he must be pretty old. His hair is gray."

"I just don't know. I just don't know."

Jonathan had never heard his father sound so unsure.

"It must be a costume, huh, Dad? And a mask?"

He wanted his father to reassure him even though he was old enough to know the truth. He tried not to stare. A costume? Hardly. *Sometimes things in nature go terribly wrong.* No mask could have shifted that mangled face so that one eye stared out of the space where the hunchback's cheek should have been while the rest of his face was frozen in a permanent mass of wrinkles that barely allowed his other eye to open. And it was only some cruel trick of nature that could have shortened one arm to a mere stub. The other arm hung all out of proportion to the dwarf-sized body as if it belonged to a six-foot tall man. He'd pumped up the good arm up so that it rippled with muscles. There was even a grotesque tattoo of some exotic bird on the oversized biceps.

"Do you think he's homeless?" Jonathan whispered.

"I have no idea."

Jonathan thought about the abandoned Penny's and Al's Barber Shop. And all the people without a place to live.

"Shouldn't he be, you know, *kept* somewhere, I mean, where someone can take care of him?"

"He certainly would've been when I was a boy. They would've locked him up and thrown away the key to the door."

"You mean his mom and dad would've left him there to die?"

"No, no, they just wouldn't have let him out like this, that's all. They kept people like this behind closed doors."

"Why? To take care of them?"

"Yes, and maybe so the rest of us wouldn't have to see them."

"You mean so we wouldn't be scared?"

"Well, that, and maybe so we wouldn't have to think about – I don't know, *life*, I guess, and what it all means."

"You mean why God would let something like this happen?"

"I suppose something like that. Times are different now. Things change, you know."

"That's what mom always says."

"She does say that, doesn't she?"

The hunchback pivoted suddenly and walked right towards them.

For a long moment, father and son stood united in their horror, the boy simply a smaller version of the man. Jonathan clung to his dad's hand, the anger and hate suddenly gone. If you'd told him he was giving his father a second chance, he would've denied it. Yet he held on tight and even touched his head to his father's arm exactly as he did when he was younger.

Fred steered a path back through the maze of pumpkins and headed straight for the parking lot.

Right at the edge of the patch, Jonathan spied a large

symmetrical pumpkin.

"Please, Dad, can I have this one?"

"Now, son, it's getting late."

Oh, boy. There he goes again.

Fred caught himself then – and bent down to pick up the heavy sphere.

"Sorry, you know that? I don't mean to be cross with you."

"Yeah, I know."

As they walked back to the car, they had to pass through a large gate. On the other side stood the hunchback, his lopsided eyes focused on them. He screwed up his face in what seemed to be an effort to smile. Jonathan took his dad's free hand and squeezed it.

"He was born that way, right?" he asked as he closed the car door and sat down beside his father.

"Yes, I think so, sure, he must've been."

Jonathan was still for a long moment, trying to put his thoughts into words.

"I don't think I understand God. Do you?"

"I can't say as I do, not all the time."

"Mom believes God is always watching over us."

"I know."

Jonathan peered out of the car window.

"Then what about him?"

"I don't have all the answers, not by a long shot."

As the Ford rolled off the gravel onto the open road and picked up speed, Jonathan watched the hunchback disappear into the patch of orange.

"I guess we're pretty lucky, huh, Dad?"

"You said it, son. You said it."

There are a thousand hacking at the branches of evil to the one who is striking at the root.

Henry David Thoreau

Access Closed

Joey Dean Hale

By 5:00 p.m. the half-moon hung over the power plant lake in boredom. Jack had fished for two hours in a small cove, catching only three channel cats, none really big enough to keep, and so he gathered his gear and headed back into the trees. But on his way down the trail through the woods to the parking lot he spontaneously ducked beneath the ACCESS CLOSED sign and cautiously descended the fifty shaky wooden steps down to the water's edge. And now for the last half hour he had stood on the small unstable dock watching the tips of the rods in the light of the battery-powered lantern. It appeared he had the lake all to himself and he was not surprised. He figured most people had better things to do on Thanksgiving.

The power plant stood around the bend and beyond the light of the lantern, shadows and silhouettes all merged together, so much so that he could barely make out the tree-line on the opposite shore. Countless stars overhead hung in their fixed patterns, too dull to reflect on the surface of the lake.

The line on the rod on the left side of the lantern twitched a little and he studied the tip of the pole.

Nothing.

His thoughts shifted back to the preacher he had seen earlier at the gas station, but then the line on that left rod moved again ever so slightly. He stepped closer but the dock shifted abruptly and he staggered a little and almost stepped off into the water. Kneeling down carefully Jack took up the slack in the line, then clicked open the bail again. He liked to fish with an open bail when the fish were moving slow like this. Let em take it, he thought. Of course at this rate it was unlikely he would catch enough for a mess tonight, unless he just happened to hook a couple of dandies real soon.

The small dock was merely three glorified pallets fastened together with large rusty iron hinges like he used to see on old barn doors. Of course there had to be something beneath the pallets, small barrels or possibly heavy Styrofoam, keeping the entire thing afloat, though now the first section sat tilted with one side sloping down into the water, and he wondered if the whole dock might not just break away, setting him on a very slow but dangerous voyage about the lake. True, the water on this side ran pleasantly warm from out of the power plant into the lake – he'd washed the putrid cheese bait from his hands after he'd baited up – but if he toppled off this junky contraption he would more than likely drown, weighted down by his long underwear and jacket and his overalls and rubber boots.

The fish bumping his line had either given up or stolen his bait, and as he reeled in the line he could feel the empty treble hook trailing effortlessly through the water. He opened the small jar and dug out a chunk of the bait with his forefinger and rolled the stinking conglomeration into a ball between his palms before pressing the glob onto the three barbs of the hook. Cut shad was what he needed, but the bait shop had been closed for the holiday.

He swished his hands in the warm lake again and dried them on the rag from his back pocket before he cast, this time just a little further out and to the west. He imagined himself falling off this dock, his rubber boots and pockets filling with lake water as he flailed pointlessly in the darkness.

He turned his attention to the sky above, attempting to locate any constellations, though besides the Little Dipper he did not know them by name. And he was not one hundred percent sure the Little Dipper was actually a constellation. He saw one he thought might be the scorpion. Or maybe the crab. Probably nothing. Just another random cluster of stars.

The preacher, Kenneth Schote, was an old man now, thin

gray hair, large almost comedic glasses, a bulky insulated coat. At first, when Schote pulled up on the other side of the gas pump and crawled out of his Lincoln, he did not see Jack. And initially Jack thought about heckling Preacher Schote for his own amusement, but then he wondered how he could think such a thing. What's the matter with me? he thought. Why can't I just keep quiet and pump my gas like a normal human being?

But the preacher commented about the price of gas and how it was hard on those traveling during this holiday and then he said, "You look familiar."

"Yeah, I used to go to your church when I was a kid."

At the lake a sudden heavy crunching in the dry leaves back behind him caused Jack to jerk around, quaking the dock once again. A coon, he rationalized. Or it could've been a deer.

He listened intently.

Nothing.

Then again – the strange bustling moved across the steep bank to the left of the steps he had earlier descended. Whatever it was seemed too noisy to be a coon. And too obvious to be a deer. And why would a deer attempt such an incline when there were much better places to approach the water's edge for a drink?

He could not make out the wooden steps, not to mention the varmint making all the racket, so he retrieved the small flashlight from his tackle box and shined the weak beam in the direction of the noise.

Nothing.

He shined on down as far as the light would allow. To the left, then to the right. Up and down the bank.

Nothing.

A few months ago there had been an email going around with a picture of a panther some guy had supposedly killed in this region of southern Illinois, but it just so happened about a year ago he had gotten the exact same picture from a different person and that panther was supposedly shot in Missouri, so

131

he assumed it had just been one of those Internet legends. A hoax to liven up the general population's mundane existence.

But what if this really was a panther?

For some reason he was reminded of a comic book he had once read as a kid while waiting for a haircut in O'Neil's Barbershop. After being attacked by a black panther Tarzan had quickly maneuvered around until he held the cat in a full-nelson, his legs locked around the beast's ribcage. Beads of sweat broke out across the Lord of the Jungle's forehead as he gritted his teeth, every muscle flexed and straining, and eventually he snapped that panther's neck. But Jack was in no shape to wrestle a panther. He'd had a hard enough time trying to wallow down all those steps with his fishing equipment.

Suddenly the fattest possum he had ever seen waddled into the light. It was so long and heavy it resembled a potbellied pig. He thought, God, I get around about like that possum. He stuck the flashlight in his back pocket and looked down at the poles in the lantern light.

Nothing.

After the typical niceties the preacher had ask him where he was off to, and when he had answered, "Fishing at the lake," Schote suggested the evening best be spent with what family Jack had left.

"Whatever happened to your buddy Greg? Now weren't you guys related?"

"I don't ever see him unless he needs something."

"Well, that's a shame."

"Speaking of a shame," Jack said, "I guess you knew Paul Buerster died?"

Schote leaned in close to Jack. "Now that was a shame. And such a great loss."

"Yeah, I went to school with his son Henry. He figured you'd be at his dad's funeral since you guys were such good friends and all."

"Yes, Paul and I were good friends; unfortunately I had

other obligations that day."

Jack thought about letting it go but could not. "Yeah, I knew you were friends because . . . well . . . this is weird, but I remember seeing you talking to him in the DMV on my sixteenth birthday. Back when I got my first driver's license."

"Really? Well now, that must've been quite some time ago."

"About twenty-four years or so."

He smiled. "You have an amazing memory."

"Well . . . I found it odd since Paul was Catholic and that one summer at The Christian Church Camp you said that Catholics would all go to Hell for worshipping Mary instead of just Jesus."

"Oh now, I think you're misquoting me."

"No. We were in the chapel and you'd been playing your saxophone. And I remember thinking, 'That ain't right.' I mean, half my friends in grade school were Catholic, and I didn't think they were going to Hell. But really, I didn't think it was right for you to say that to a bunch of kids anyway. Even then, I didn't think it was right."

"Well, I certainly don't remember saying that." His face had turned serious. Not angry, but very concerned. "I sure hope that's not why you stopped attending church services."

"It wasn't just the one thing, I don't guess."

Jack stooped down and held his watch over close to the light of the lantern though he was really in no hurry to be any place else. Slowly reeling in each line, he relished the dark surroundings. The blue-black sky. The dull stars in the distance. The faint tree-line across the smooth lake surface. He clutched the rods and lantern in one hand and the tackle box and bait in the other and laboriously climbed the wooden stairs.

When he reached his truck, parked alone in the shadows, he started the engine to let the heater warm up the cab then loaded his gear in the back before relieving himself by the dumpster.

According to the thermometer on his dash the temperature

had dropped to 29 degrees; he rubbed his hands together while steering across the empty parking spaces with one knee. He thought about the radio but drove on out of the conservation area in silence.

He had asked the preacher, "So did you ever try to save his soul?"

His pump clicked off as he stood there facing Jack. "Who's that?"

"Paul Buerster. If you seriously thought he was going to Hell, shouldn't you have tried to save him?"

"I really don't remember saying that about Catholics, but to be honest . . ." Again Brother Schote stepped in close. "When someone believes something so strongly, when they've been brought up and raised to have certain beliefs, it's very hard to change their mind. And Paul was such a good man, who worked hard in his own church, and rather than try to change someone, it's usually just best to be their friend and love them as they are." He pulled out his billfold and said, "Now I need to go pay for my gas and get on home, but I want to invite you back into the church. Maybe after services we could continue this conversation."

Now out on the blacktop Jack passed several houses, the driveways packed with cars and trucks, the lights on in every room. Families catching that second or third round of turkey and dressing. Football and fire roaring in the living rooms. Several already had Christmas lights and trees illuminating their front windows.

He wondered what it would be like to be inside those homes. How did the people interact at times like these?

Christina Weidner, a girl he had dated back in the '80's, lived up here by the lake, though he had not spoken to her in years. She had married Kyle Iffert and they now owned the very same house where Christina grew up, and Jack imagined dropping by there tonight, cold and dirty and reeking of fish and cheese flavored bait.

Kyle and Christina's relatives would whisper nervously

among themselves as he stood in the doorway, refusing all offers of food and drink or even a chair. And just when they thought the situation could get no more awkward he would mention that right here at this doorstep, on this very threshold, after each of their dates, he had kissed Christina goodnight. Had made out with her passionately. And he could still remember how her lips tasted like cherry Jolly Ranchers. And how she smelled like some rare angelic flower – a sweet faint sentimental fragrance – and he would ask Christina if she still wore that same perfume.

Alone now in his truck he laughed at how absurd that scene would be. Like a cheesy skit on television. But at least it would give their family something to talk about. Even next year and maybe even for years to come. It might even become something of a tradition for them.

In the future after the turkey and dressing and pumpkin pie and everything else they thought Pilgrims might indulge in, Kyle and Christina Iffert's extended family might just gather around the fireplace and recall that one Thanksgiving when Jack had shown up unexpectedly, smelling like fish and cheese bait. Asking about Christina's old perfume like a common psychopath.

He drove back into Wabash City with no specific destination, cruising down Main like a teenager. On the north end the streets were dead and no businesses open. Besides the two bars and the grocery store most buildings stood permanently closed and empty with broken windows and burned out lights. The park stood barren, void of those oaks and elms and maples uprooted by the last tornado and reminding everyone every day that this town used to be something much better. A few houses on the south end had several lights and cars in the driveway, and at the end of town Jack was surprised to find the gas station not only open but still fairly busy. Three cars and a pickup were filling up at the pumps and five other vehicles were parked against the front curb. Through the window he could see several customers lined up at the counter.

He couldn't decide if what the preacher had said earlier was a cop-out or if the old man really believed it. He wondered why they needed so many different churches in one small town when they all said there was only one God. He figured that probably wasn't a very original thought, but then again he wasn't sure he'd ever had a truly original idea. He tried to remember one original thought and came up with nothing.

He thought about the preacher, and he considered his own soul as he headed south on out of town where there was nothing but dead empty fields and leafless trees and the river weaving through the darkness.

Odd

Roberta Allen

In Egypt with a British adventure travel group, I was considered odd for wearing pajama bottoms that did not look like pajama bottoms that I had bought at Old Navy before the trip. I was sure they would be cool in the heat and would not be recognized as pajama bottoms unless I said they were, which I made the mistake of doing.

I was soon sorry about this though I need not have been, since most of the people on the tour, especially young and inexperienced travelers, did not last long in Egypt. Like the victims in that famous Agatha Christie mystery that disappear one by one or, in this case, two by two, we seemed to lose at least a couple of people every day. First to go were two plastic-sandaled girls of seventeen who boarded the train with us in Cairo but never made it to Aswan. They flew home next morning it was said though I do not remember by whom.

We had not yet met Bob, our guide, a first-time tour leader and former London cook, who knew less than nothing about Egypt. Moments after his arrival in the hotel lobby in Aswan, he sent us off in a caravan of cabs that stopped along the highway outside town. The drivers motioned us out.

"What's here?" I asked, standing with the others before large slabs of stone.

The drivers shrugged; they did not speak English. Under boiling sun, as we climbed over rocks, looking for something – anything – that might merit our attention, a Brit in the group who called herself a Physical Geographer and had her Rough Guide handy, pointed out a giant obelisk partly cut in the granite quarry.

Back in Aswan, the bus had just left the hotel when someone – other than Bob – noticed the Scottish teacher running after us. A girl from Manchester said, "That Bob is in way over his head."

Bob was happiest lying on deck in the *felluca*, sleeping or reading a soggy American novel. He let the sullen Nubian crew take charge. At night, Bob and the Nubians crept under mosquito nets to sleep while we slept under the sky at the mercy of mosquitoes.

At dawn before the others awoke, I took long walks by the tall reeds along the shore and inland on dirt paths through palm groves with ripe dates and coconuts, unfamiliar flowers, fields of corn and sugar cane, grazing cattle and canals gleaming with sun while herons, egrets, doves, bee-eaters, kingfishers, and birds unfamiliar to me, crisscrossed the cloudless sky, calling to one another. *This is the real Egypt!* I thought and breathed in the potent perfume of flowers. Just then, a man rose from the bushes a distance away. I tried to keep calm and continue my walk but after only a few steps I told myself, *Don't be an ass!* I raced back to the safety of the waiting boat. Didn't I join a tour of Egypt to avoid such dangers?

At night the *felluca* docked near shore. This was not the case during the day when we made bathroom stops. The phrase "walking the plank" and the word "bathroom" assumed new meanings. My fear of heights made descending the long, narrow wobbly wooden board over stagnant muddy water – probably rife with parasites – the equivalent of walking a tightrope in the upper reaches of a circus tent. The Nubians looked on while a tour mate helped me down. On shore, the pit Bob dug could be anywhere and, like a children's game, required a search since he conveniently disappeared after digging it.

The day the Nubians provided a make-shift *potty* was not much better. Perched on the side of a rather steep hill above a village, the contraption, which consisted of a rotted board with a round hole in the center, held up by four sticks behind a little cloth skirt, required us to sit at a severe slant while we did our business, watching water buffalo wading below. Despite my objections, the Nubians refused to let us step back on board unless we washed our feet first in buckets of dark water the crew had scooped from the river while we were gone.

An officious British magistrate of fifty-something, named Antoinette, an experienced traveler like myself, laughed at me when I, alone in the group, declined a swim the Nubians allowed us one day, in 115 degree heat. Not that 115 degree heat was exceptional. We were kept informed of every degree change by one of two Long Island Ladies, as I called them, though only one was from Long Island. Old college room-mates, both sixty, they made yearly trips together. The *real* Long Island Lady had a thermometer in one of the many pockets of her safari vest and clutched a thick notebook with multi-colored tabs where she had written down and alphabetically categorized before the tour everything she could possibly need to know in Egypt – or so she thought.

How had she managed to overlook *bilharzia?* I wondered, as I warned them all before their swim about the parasitic illness caused by worms that live in snails found in the Nile. "They burrow into human flesh to lay their eggs," I told them, but no one listened to the woman wearing pajama bottoms.

Whether it was the water, the heat, the unpasteurized ice cream I warned them not to eat when we stopped in a village, or the fish the Nubians left stinking in the sun each day before cooking, the group was drastically reduced in size after a few days on the river though the magistrate and her daughter's bouts with illness were brief, and the couple from Alberta taking doxycycline daily, which I warned them would kill good bacteria as well as bad, did not get sick at all.

By all accounts, I should not have been spared the fate of those who were no longer with us, having picked a strange green fruit one day from a bush along the Nile and, after tearing it open, lived to describe the milky substance and silky white seeds inside which the Nubians claimed was so toxic,

Antoinette told me later, that touching it should have killed me.

Nine of us remained to scream our way down the road in two speeding cabs on the harrowing ride from Edfu to Luxor, which prompted Antoinette to say to Bob who was seated upfront beside our driver, "Can you tell him to make the ride a little bit less hair-raising?" In a flat voice, Bob replied without turning his head that this was the driver's revenge for the paltry tips we had given the Nubians.

Among the survivors were the Long Island Ladies. In Luxor, when the real Long Island Lady said to her *dear* friend, "You know in Egypt when Harry drank coke from a can like you just did, he developed painful pus-filled sores all over his mouth that didn't heal for months."

Still holding the empty coke can, the Midwest Long Island Lady looked horrified and yelled, "*Why are you telling me this now?*" Her frightened face made me burst out laughing, which did not endear me to them or to the others.

What a relief it was to leave the frantic tourist-mobbed sites of Luxor, Karnak, Valley Of The Kings, and Hapshepsut's Temple, and board an air-conditioned bus without Bob on an add-on extension to the trip across hundreds of miles of uninhabited sand and rock in the Western Desert even though our new leader, James, from California, was nearly as clueless as Bob had been. A young and inventive Egyptian guide named Wael accompanied us on the way to several desert oases with stories about a deadly snake that could leap thirty feet in the air. Our armed police escort which protected us from pirate raids was the only other vehicle on the highway.

North of the first oases, Karga, where we stopped for the night, was the ancient Bagawat Necropolis rising on a ridge with 263 mud brick chapels used for Christian burials from the 3rd to 7th centuries, my guide book said, as I wandered off from the group to explore dozens of them on my own, disbelieving Wael's warnings about poisonous creatures hiding inside the vaulted ruins, which were rife with graffiti, some dating from Roman times. Was it my imagination or did Wael look a bit disappointed when I returned intact?

After two nights in El-Karga and Dakhla, with its medieval mud brick village of Al Qasr, we drove with Bedouins in battered 4-wheel drive vehicles through trackless rock and sand and stopped in what seemed to me the middle of nowhere.

While waiting for the vehicle to return, that was depositing two sick tour mates to the nearest Bedouin outpost so we could resume our journey, I began talking to Mohammed, one of the drivers. Despite his bad English we seemed to understand each other. Wearing pajama bottoms as usual – I had several pairs – which the Bedouin of course did not recognize as pajama bottoms, I climbed alongside him, this time surprisingly unafraid, up a steep stony hill. At the top, we sat down and he told me about his wealthy father and that he was one of sixty-four children. "I have two wives." he said. I do not recall how many wives his father had. I only recall looking out over the vastness of the desert, believing that Mohammed and I were the only human beings in the entire world, and that the entire world was nothing more than sand and stone. And the sand and stone were alive with a pulsing life all their own, more beautiful in their aliveness than anything I had ever seen. My eyes embraced the myriad forms. Like the browns and grays and purples and mustards and mauves that dissolved at the horizon, the forms, too, gradually gave themselves up and hugged the earth's edge.

It was only when my eyes wandered that I noticed down below the little figures of Antoinette, her daughter, the Long Island Ladies and the couple from Alberta. I did not know then that my brief awakening on the hill was only a prelude to the deeper awareness I would have in the White Desert where, after a night in a Bedouin camp, we spent the day wandering in a white chalky world of huge unearthly sculptures that could only have been carved by God. The great stones rose in profusion from a dusty white floor strewn with fossilized shells and corals from a long vanished sea and thousands of small but heavy black iron pyrites resembling broken twigs. I bumbled around, drunk with wonder, almost getting lost, collecting specimens in disbelief, making my tour mates laugh, as I held in my hands those weighted morsels.

Later, when the others, with sleeping bags like mine but also without tents, scattered in all directions to spend the night wherever they wanted, as the guide had *ordered* us to do, I, the only one without a partner, chose not to move, and was rewarded by the rare sight of a jackal, a small nocturnal creature, as delicate and transparent as a glass figurine. Innocent and unafraid, it watched me while suckling the string of my sleeping bag cover before vanishing like a dream. While I handled the still moist string, Antoinette came running out of nowhere to inform me that the jackal was probably rabid, which meant that I, too, would probably get the disease.

Her prediction, however, failed to spoil my time alone with the stars which either lowered themselves or lifted me up, as I lay in pajama bottoms over my sleeping bag in the heat. While the stars and I stared at one another and I felt safe from the imaginary leaping snake and the real horned viper, from scorpions, beetles, and larger creatures whose tracks I would see in the sand circling my head when I awoke next morning, I was unaware that a screeching 4-wheel-drive emergency vehicle with flashing lights, which was seen and heard by all the others, had come for the violently retching couple from Alberta and taken them away.

Biographical Notes & Publication Acknowledgments

Roberta Allen is the author of eight books, including the novel, *The Dreaming Girl*, republished in 2011 (Ellipsis Press) and three story collections. She has just completed a novel called *In This Room*. A visual artist as well, her work has been exhibited worldwide and is in the collection of The Metropolitan Museum. www.robertaallen.com

W.C. Bamberger is the author, editor or translator of more than a dozen books, including the novel *On the Back Stretch* and his translation of *Two Draft Essays from 1918 by Gershom Scholem*. He lives in Michigan.

Edie Cottrell recently retired from a career teaching English and humanities at Merritt College in Oakland, California. She grew up in San Antonio, Texas, and received her B.A. from the University of Texas, Austin, and her M.A. from the University of California, Berkeley. Recent fiction appears in *The Healing Muse* and *Proud to Be: Writing by American Warriors*. Currently, she is working on a novel.

Gary Guinn's novel, *A Late Flooding Thaw*, was published in 2005. His work has appeared in *The Midwest Poetry Review*, *The Bryant Literary Review*, *Ghoti*, *Elder Mountain: a Journal of Ozark Studies*, *The Arkansas Literary Review*, *Carve Magazine*, and others. One of his stories will appear in an anthology of Ozark Writers from The University of Arkansas Press in 2013. The story "The Scar" was published in the November 2004 issue of *Carve Magazine*.

Atar Hadari was born in Israel, raised in England. His *Songs from Bialik: Selected Poems of H.N. Bialik* (Syracuse University Press) was a finalist for the American Literary Translators' Association Award and his poems have won the Daniel Varoujan award from

New England Poetry Club, the Petra Kenney award, a Paumanok poetry award and many other prizes. His collection *Rembrandt's Bible* is forthcoming in 2013.

Joey Dean Hale, a writer and musician in the St. Louis area, has published stories in several magazines, including *Pithead Chapel*, *Fried Chicken and Coffee*, *Roadside Fiction*, and *Octave Magazine*, which also has his song "High Noon" posted online. In September 2012 he was the featured writer in Penduline Press.

Rivka Keren (born as Katalin Friedländer in Debrecen, Hungary, July 24, 1946) is an Israeli writer. She immigrated to Israel in 1957 and studied painting, philosophy, literature and clinical psychology. So far, she published fifteen books for adults, adolescents and children, won numerous literary prizes and has been translated to English, German, Spanish, Russian, Hungarian and Braille. Her work is a study of human nature, the destructiveness of evil and revenge, and the power of hope and love. Currently she is working on a new novel, set in the first century in Italy. Rivka resides in Gainesville, Florida, and she is married with two children. The story here is a self-contained chapter from the novel *Mortal Love* first published in Hebrew (Ahavah Anusha) by Am Oved, Hasifria Laam, 1992. Published in English by YouWriteOn.com, 2008. Further information: en.wikipedia.org/wiki/Rivka_Keren

The stories, poetry, and humor of **Larry Lefkowitz** have been widely published in the U.S., Israel, and Britain in print, online, and in anthologies in a variety of genres. Lefkowitz immigrated to Israel in 1972 and also has had stories published which he translated into Hebrew.

Michele Merens is a writer with short stories published in *Third Wednesday, Plum Hamptons, Inkwell, Thema, Lilith* and *Crawdad* and in three anthologies; there are also play and monologue publications. She is a winner of a 2008 Puffin Foundation Grant for *The Lion's Den*, a DVD production which is archived at the

Wisconsin Veteran's Museum, Madison, WI. She is a member of the Dramatist's Guild.

Julie J. Nichols, a native of the San Francisco Bay Area, is Associate Professor of English at Utah Valley University in Orem, Utah. Her fiction and nonfiction have been published in *Sunstone; Dialogue: A Journal of Mormon Thought; The Rocky Mountain Review; The Journal for the Assembly for Expanded Learning;* and elsewhere, and her reviews appear regularly online at newpages.com.

Arthur Powers went to Brazil in 1969 as a Peace Corps Volunteer and lived most his adult life there. From 1985 to 1992, he and his wife served with the Franciscans in Tocantins, organizing subsistence farmers in a region of violent land conflicts. His collection of short stories set in Brazil, *A Hero For The People*, is forthcoming from Press 53. The story here appeared in *St. Katherine Review*, volume 2, Number 3 (September 2012).

Frank Russo has been short-listed for the Vogel/*The Australian* Literary Prize and various other prizes. His writing has appeared in *The Weekend Australian, Southerly, Transnational Literature, Blue Crow*, in various anthologies and broadcast on radio. He has a Master of Arts from the University of Technology, Sydney and is currently completing a doctorate at the University of Sydney.

Bill Scalia has published essays on literature and film in the journals *Religion and Literature, Literature/Film Quarterly*, and in the anthology *Faith and Spirituality in Masters of World Cinema*. He also edited the anthology *Classic Critical Views: Ralph Waldo Emerson*, and is currently at work on a book concerning Emersonian aesthetics, poetry, and film. Dr. Scalia teaches literature and writing at St. Mary's Seminary & University in Baltimore, Maryland.

Patty Somlo has been nominated for the Pushcart Prize three times and is the author of *From Here to There and Other Stories*. Her work has appeared in the *Los Angeles Review, the Santa Clara Review, WomenArts Quarterly,* among others, and in six anthologies, including, *Solace in So Many Words,* winner of the Next Generation Indie Book Award. The story here was previously published in *Shaking,* volume 1, on February 14, 2012.

Andrea Vojtko is a writer and artist residing in Arlington, Virginia. She has been nominated previously for a Pushcart Prize. Her fiction has appeared in the Anthology *Being Human: Call of the Wild,* the *Potomac Review, Words of Wisdom* and *Road and Travel.* She is a member of The Writer's Center in Bethesda, Maryland where she attended many fiction writing workshops. She received her degrees in mathematics, and is an avid naturalist, painter and genealogist.

—

—

ABOUT BIBLIOTEKOS

Mission and Goals: To produce books of literary merit that address important issues, complex ideas, and enduring themes. We believe in the lasting power of the written word, especially in book form. We believe in contributing to a deeper understanding of what it means to be human (individually and socially) – who we are and what we should do.

For a petit publisher, creating collections is a time-consuming and tedious process, but well worth the effort in producing books worth reading and studying for years to come. Was it in our destiny to become publishers? We are students of philosophy, literature, and history (including interest in science as it relates to human behavior). We are scholars, academics, and writers – humanists. We are not business people, but somewhere in our intellectual journey we felt more acutely than usual the joy and pain associated with writing and publishing and then made the decision to shepherd other people's work into print.

If you liked this book, read (also by Bibliotekos):

Pain and Memory: Reflections on the Strength of the Human Spirit in Suffering (2009);

Common Boundary: Stories of Immigration (2010);

Battle Runes: Writings on War (2011);

Being Human: Call of the Wild (2012).